COLORWORLD COLORING BOOK!

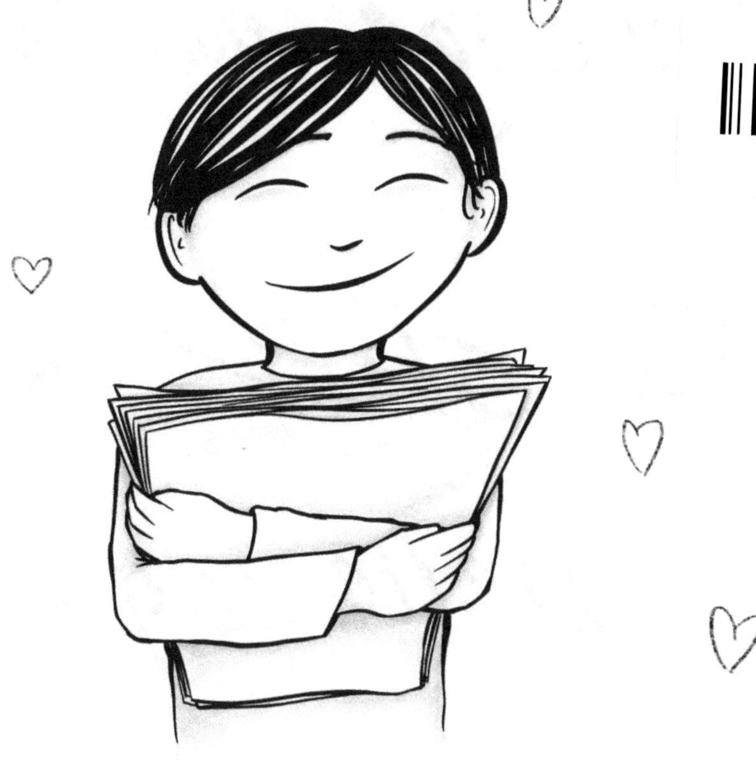

Drawings by Anthony Richichi

Colored by ____________

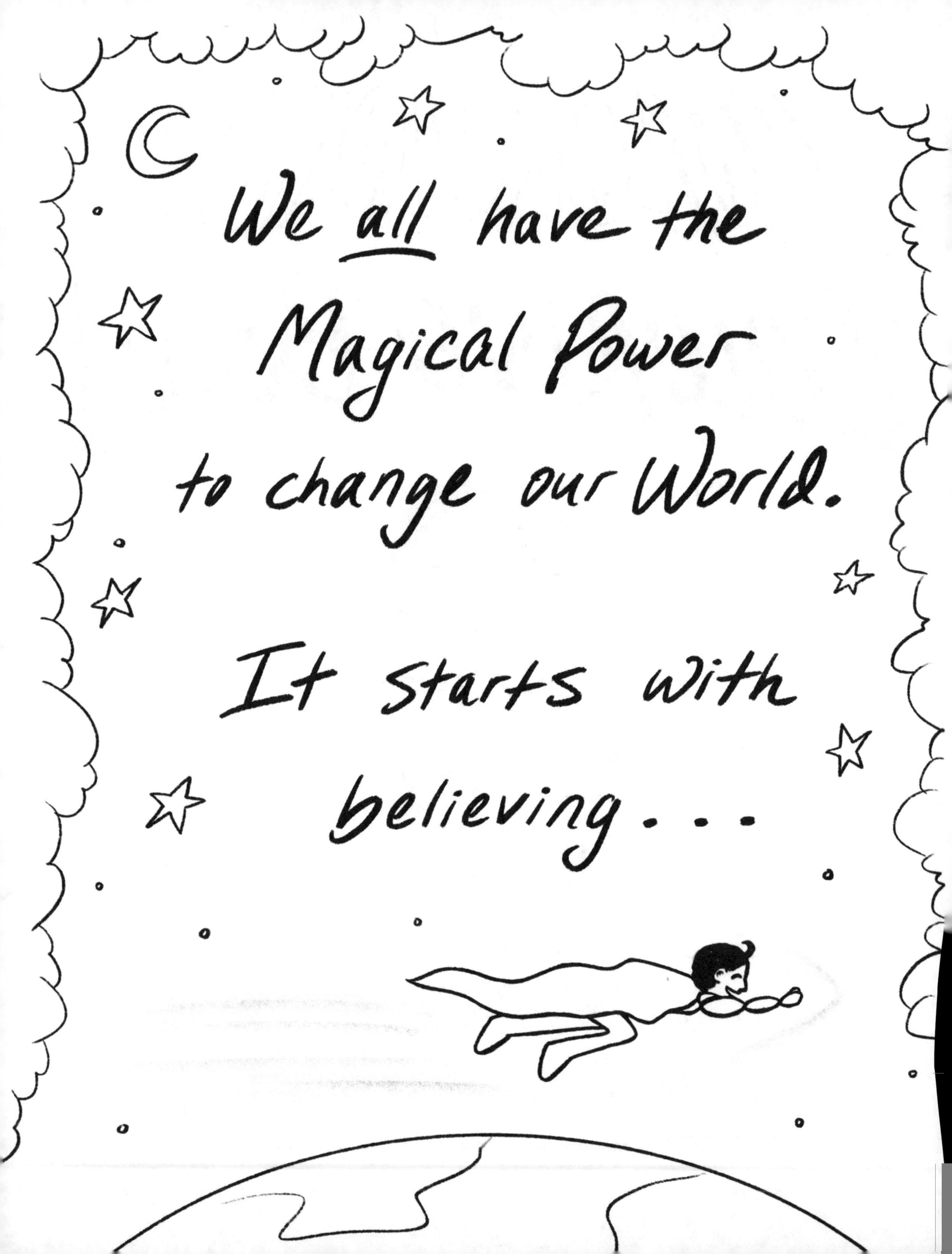

We *all* have the
Magical Power
to change our World.

It starts with
believing...

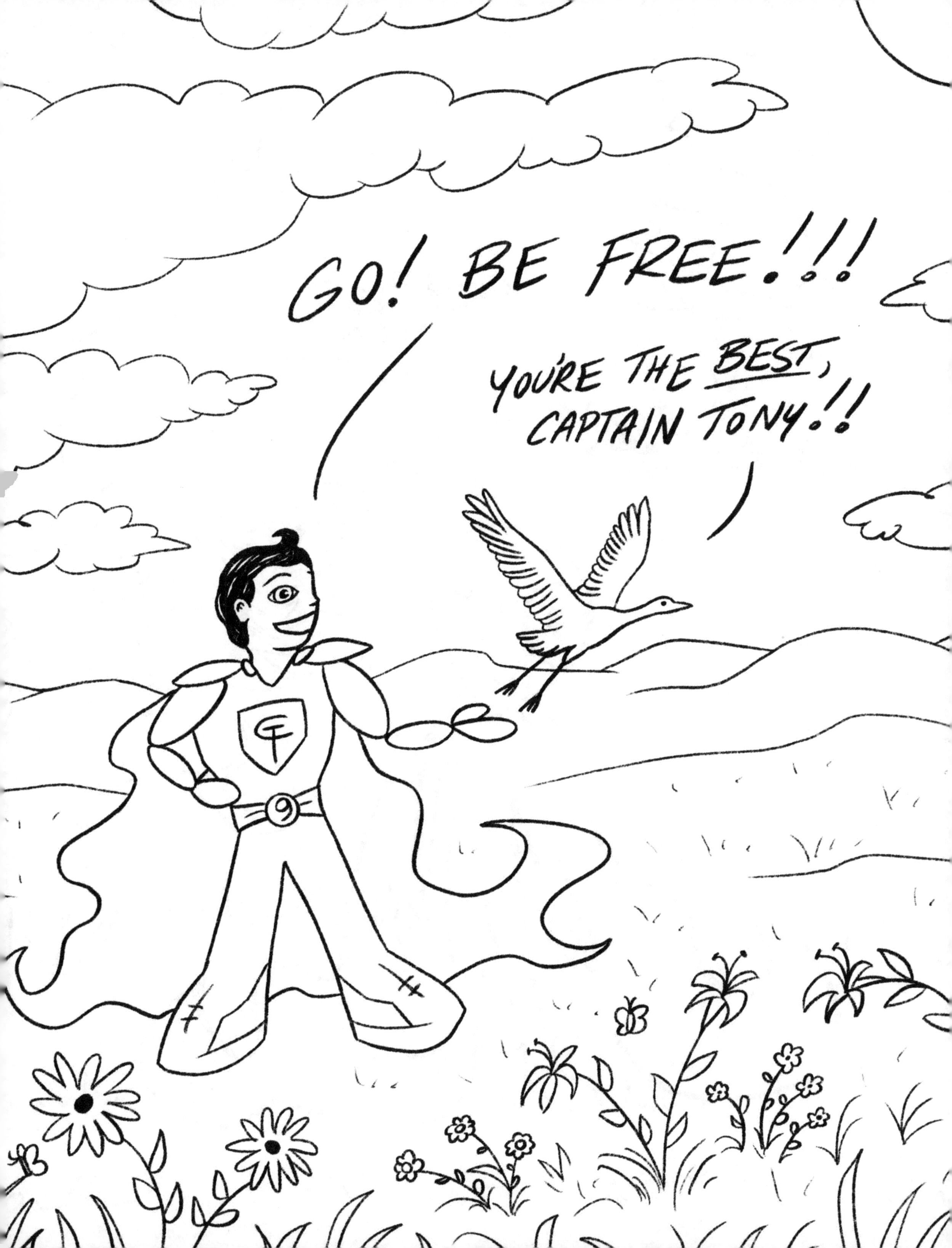
GO! BE FREE!!!
YOU'RE THE BEST, CAPTAIN TONY!!

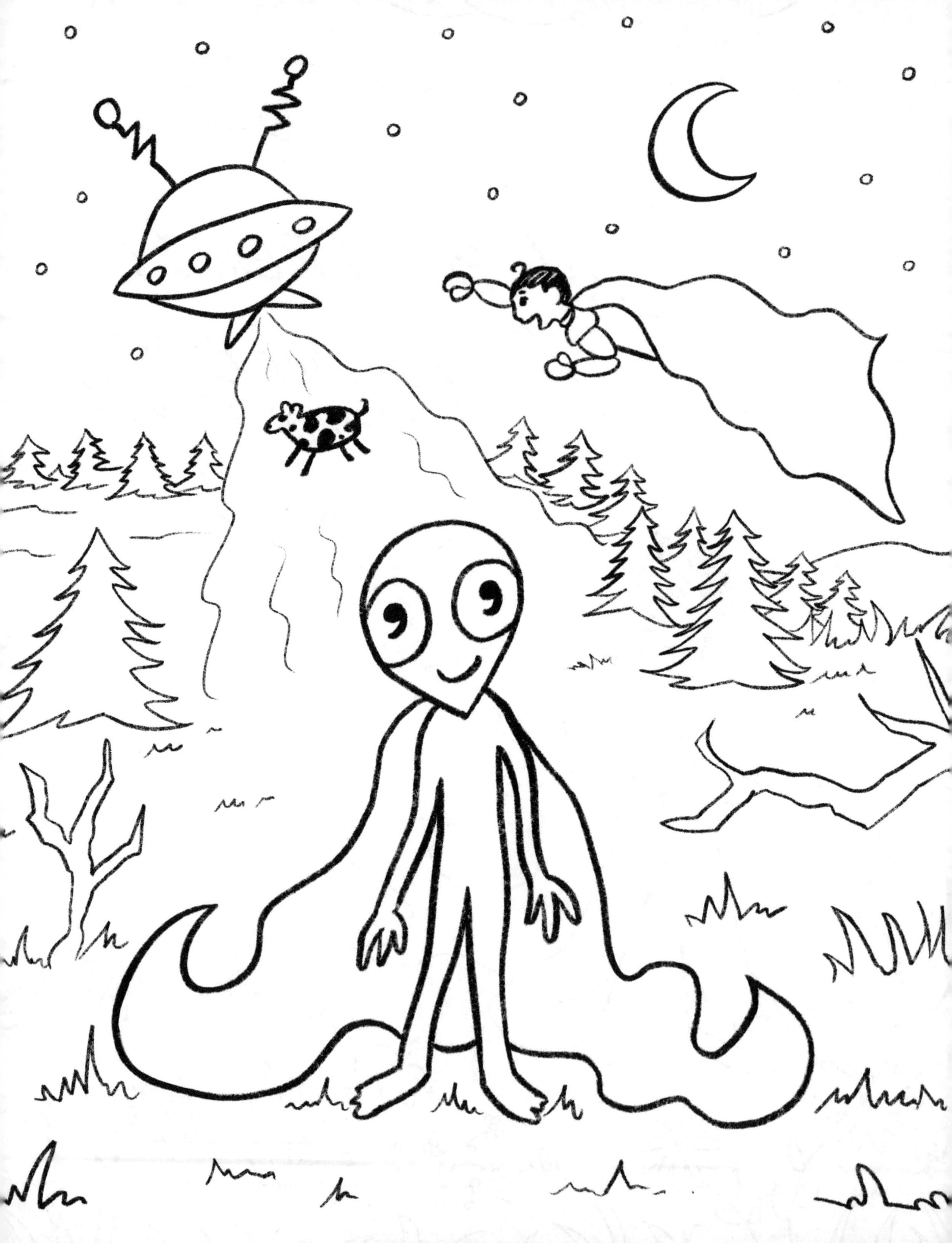

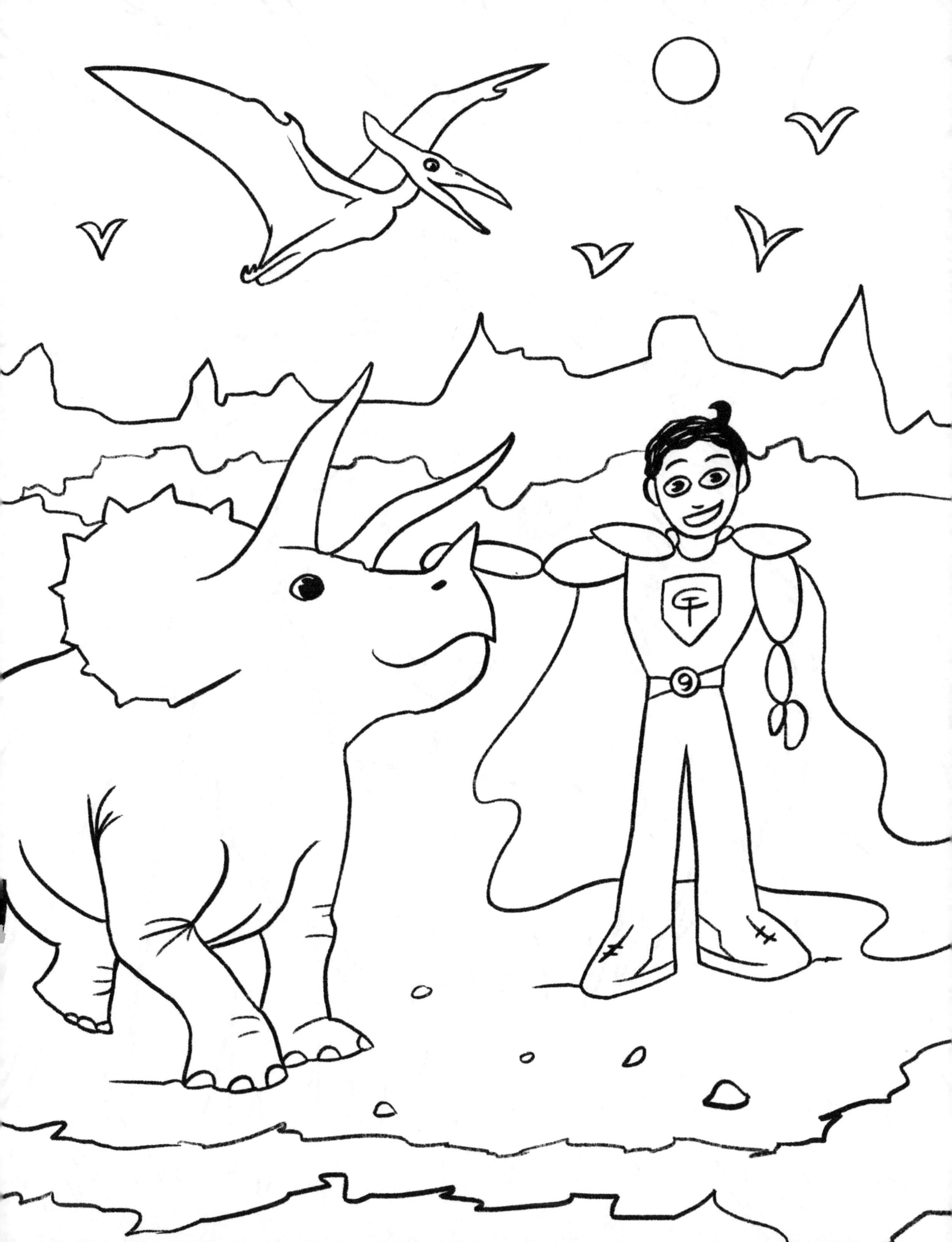

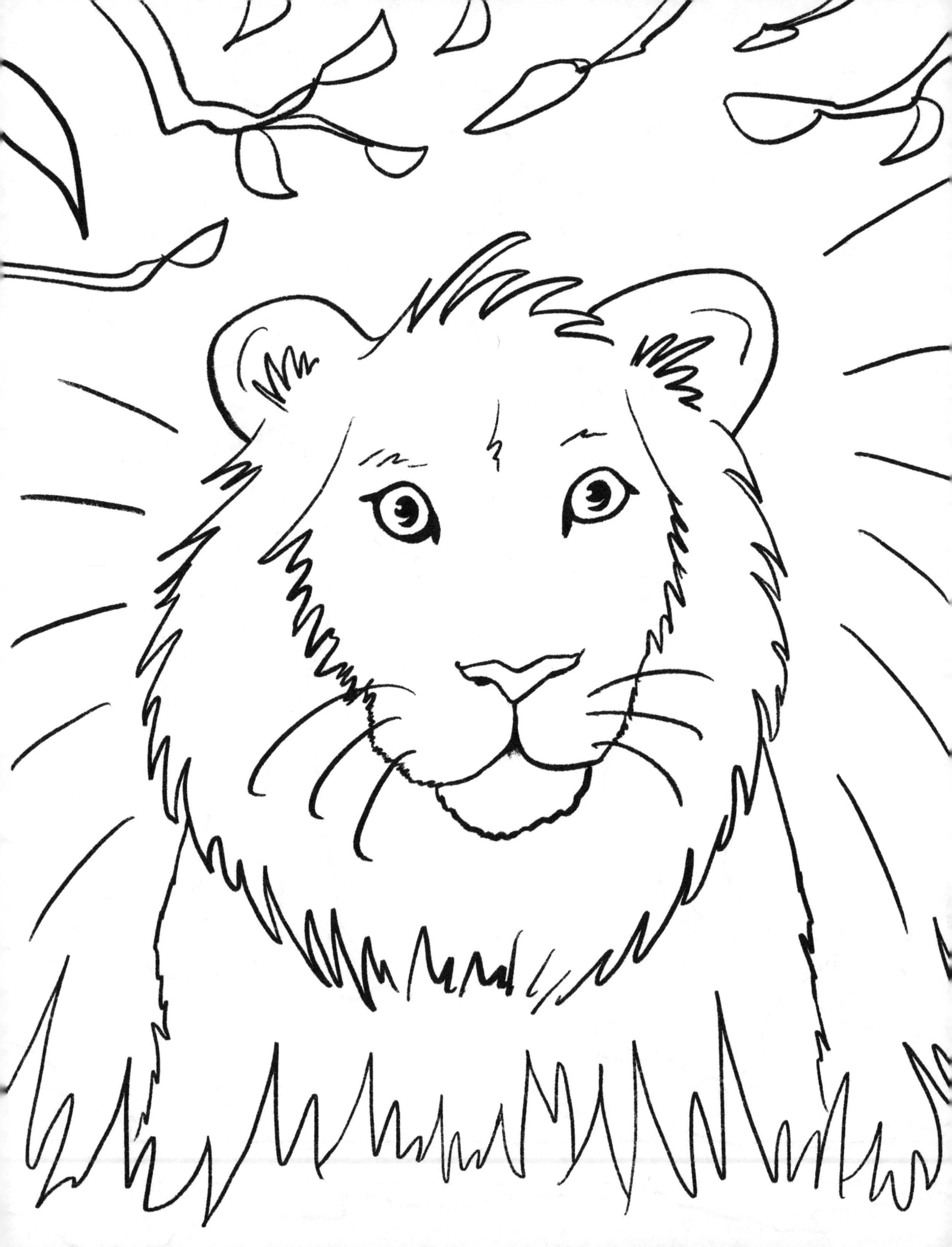

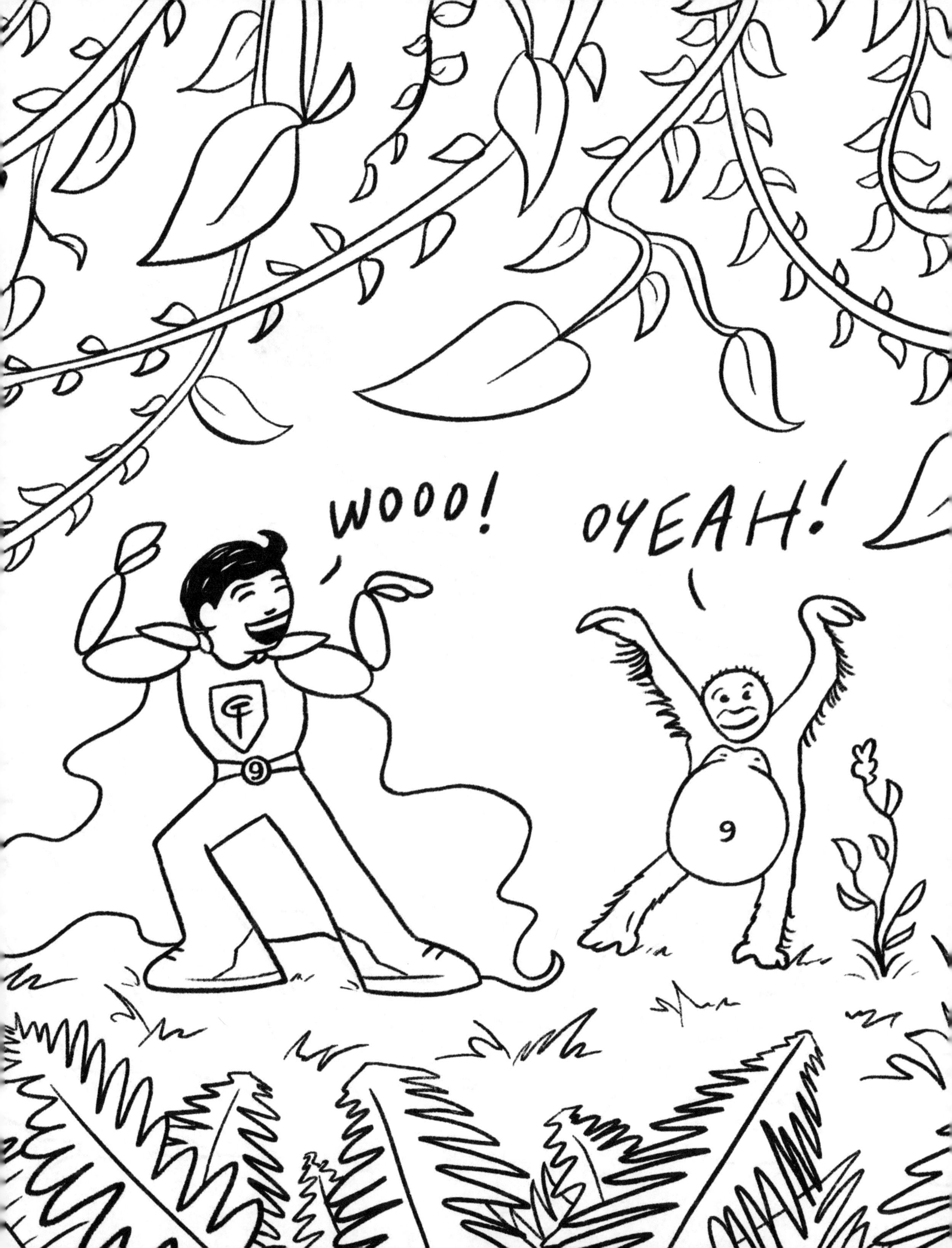
WOOO!
OYEAH!

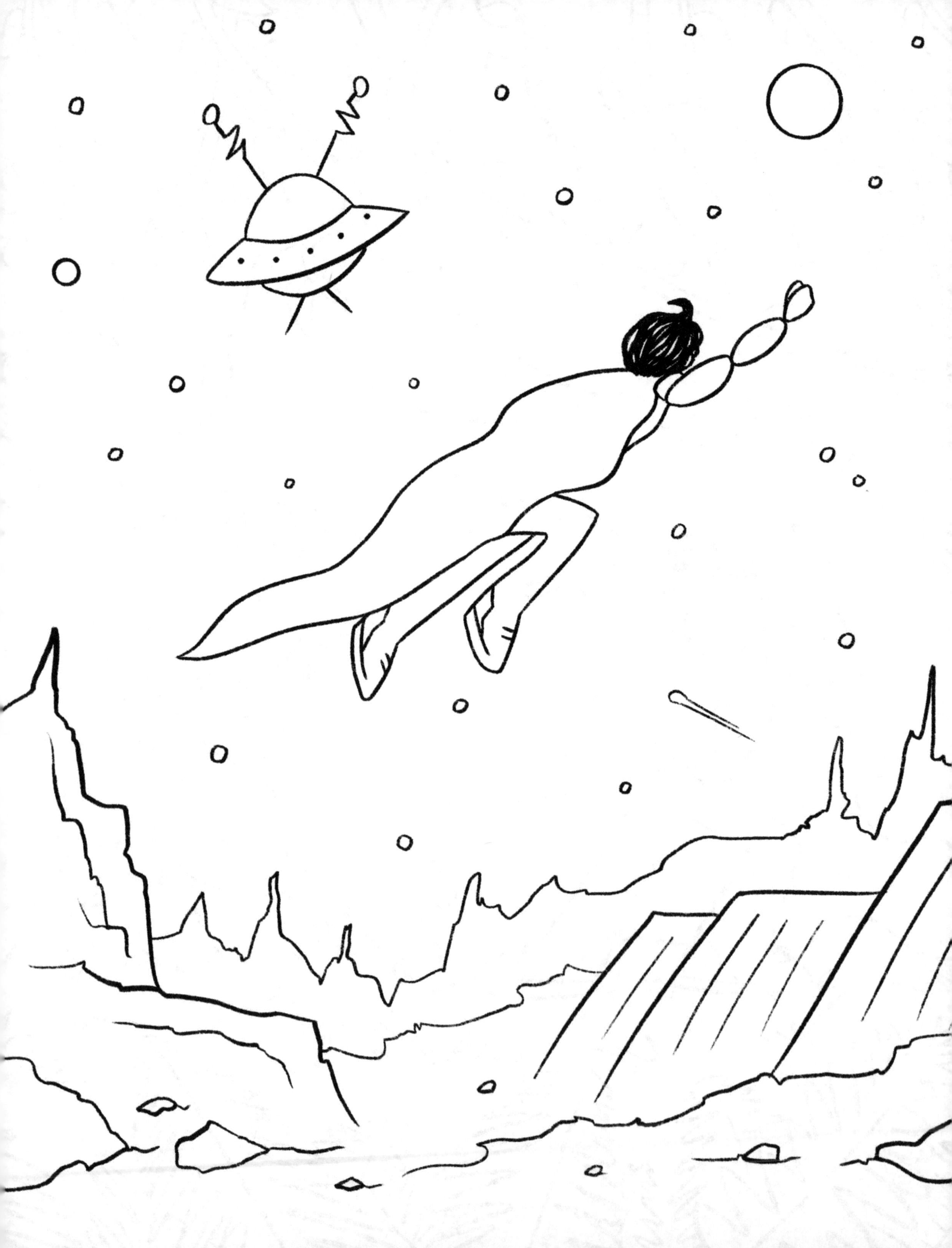

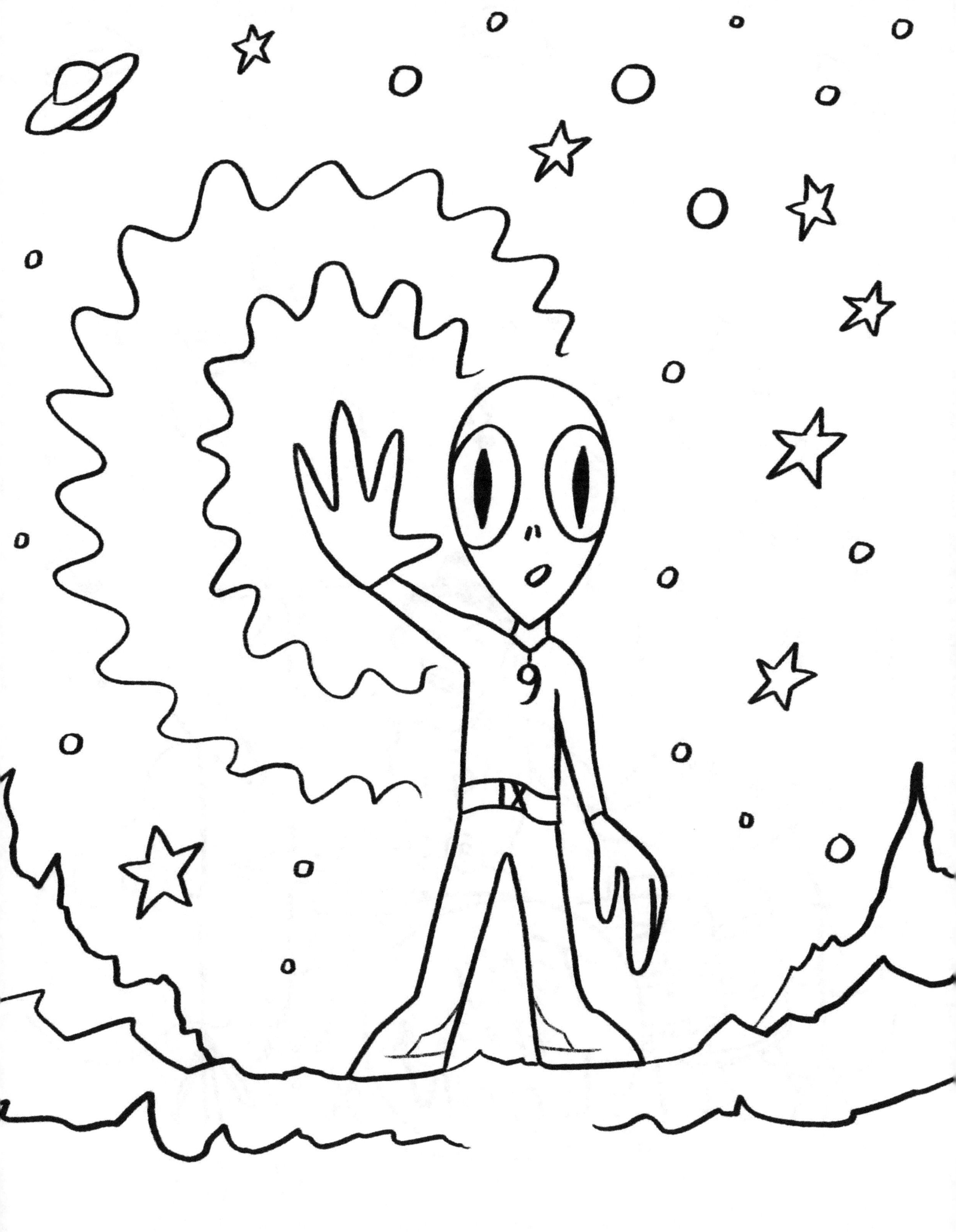
9
IX

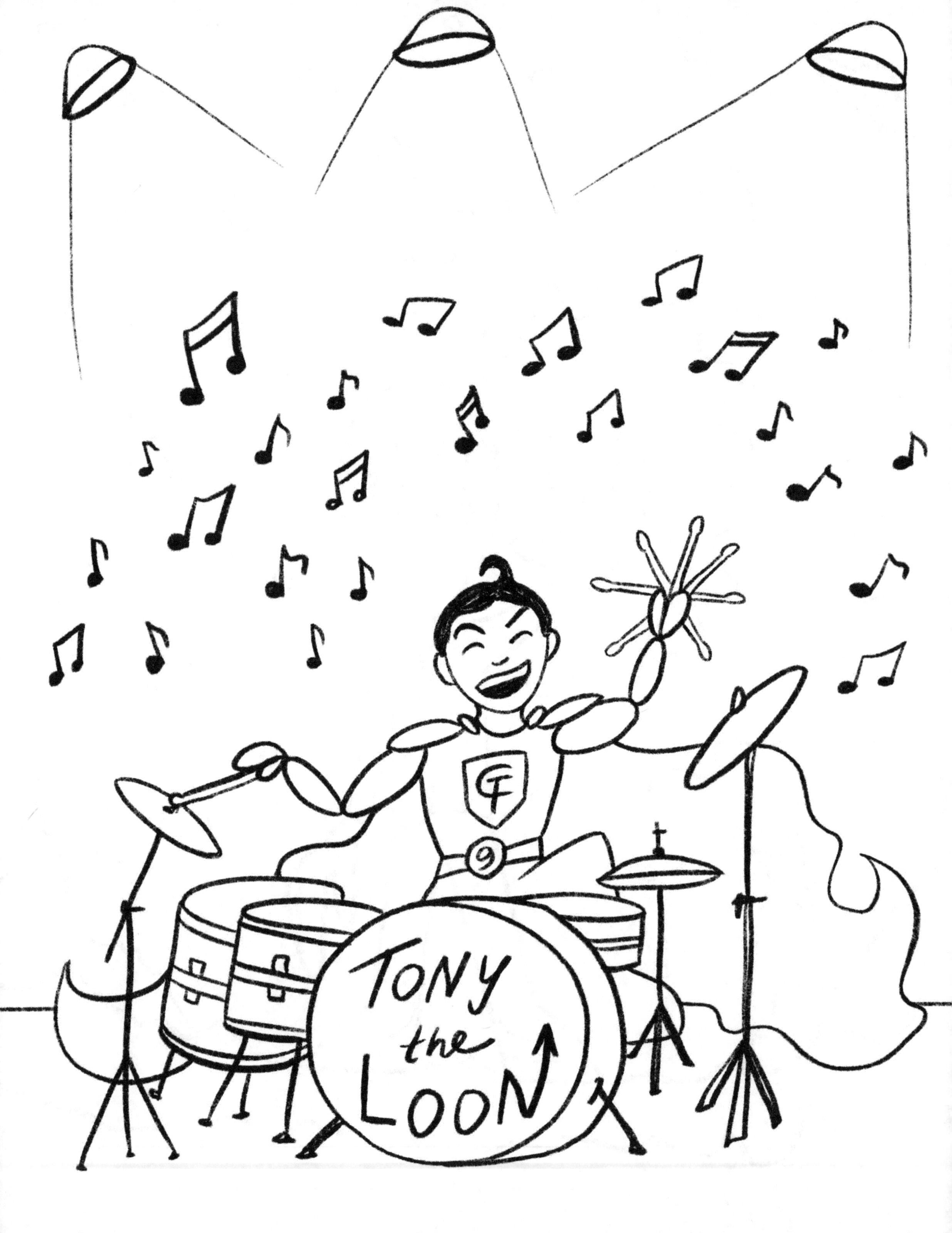
Tony the LooN

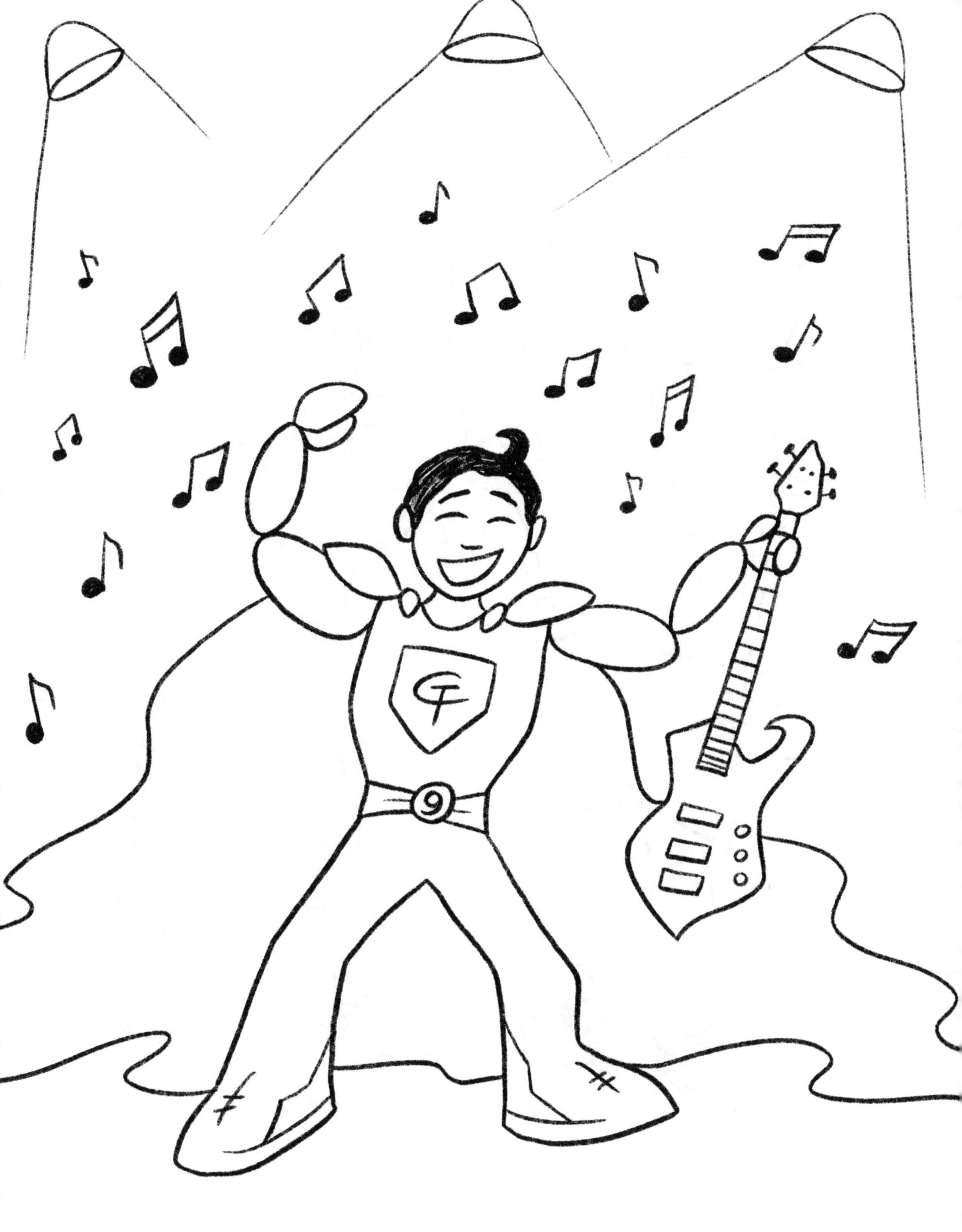

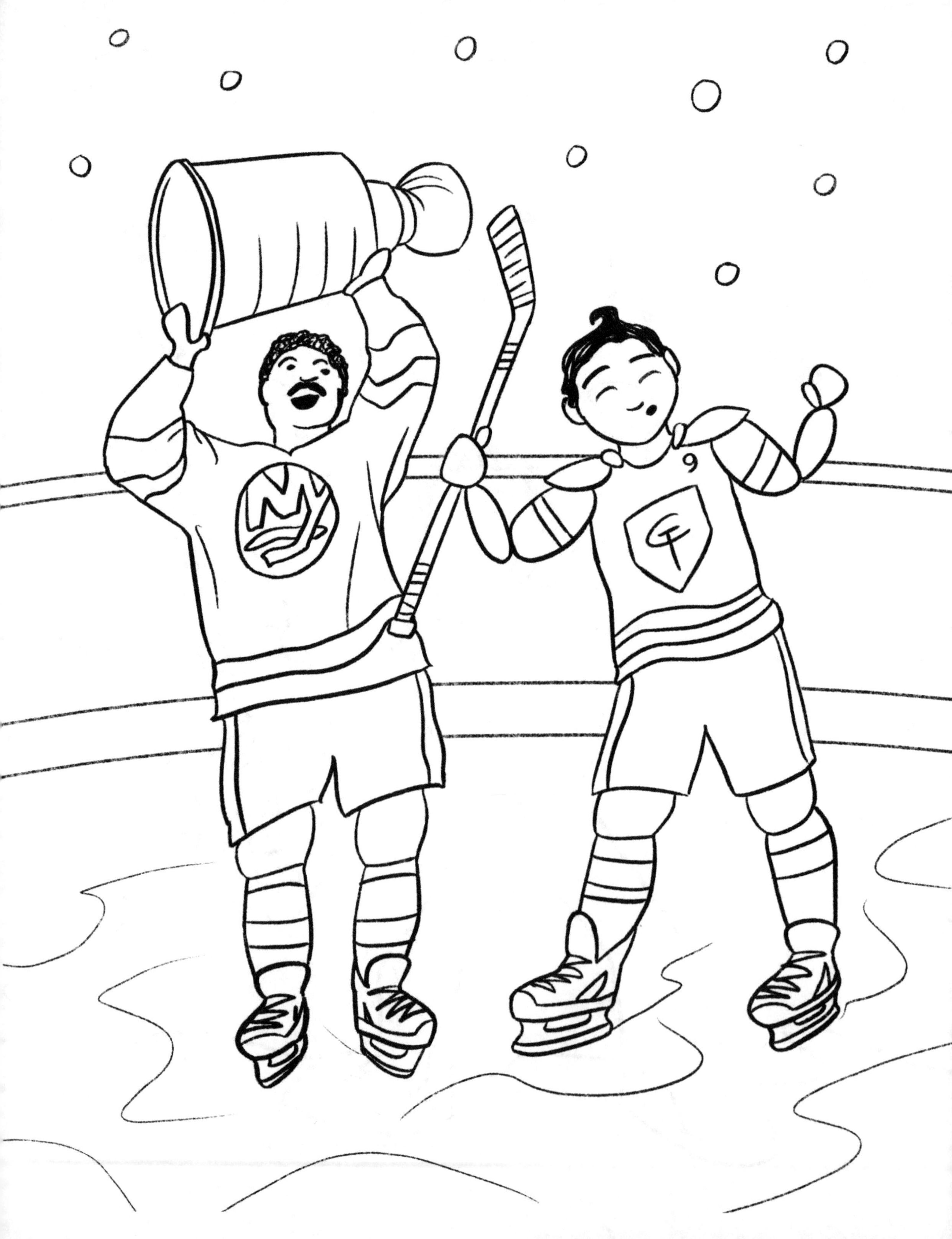

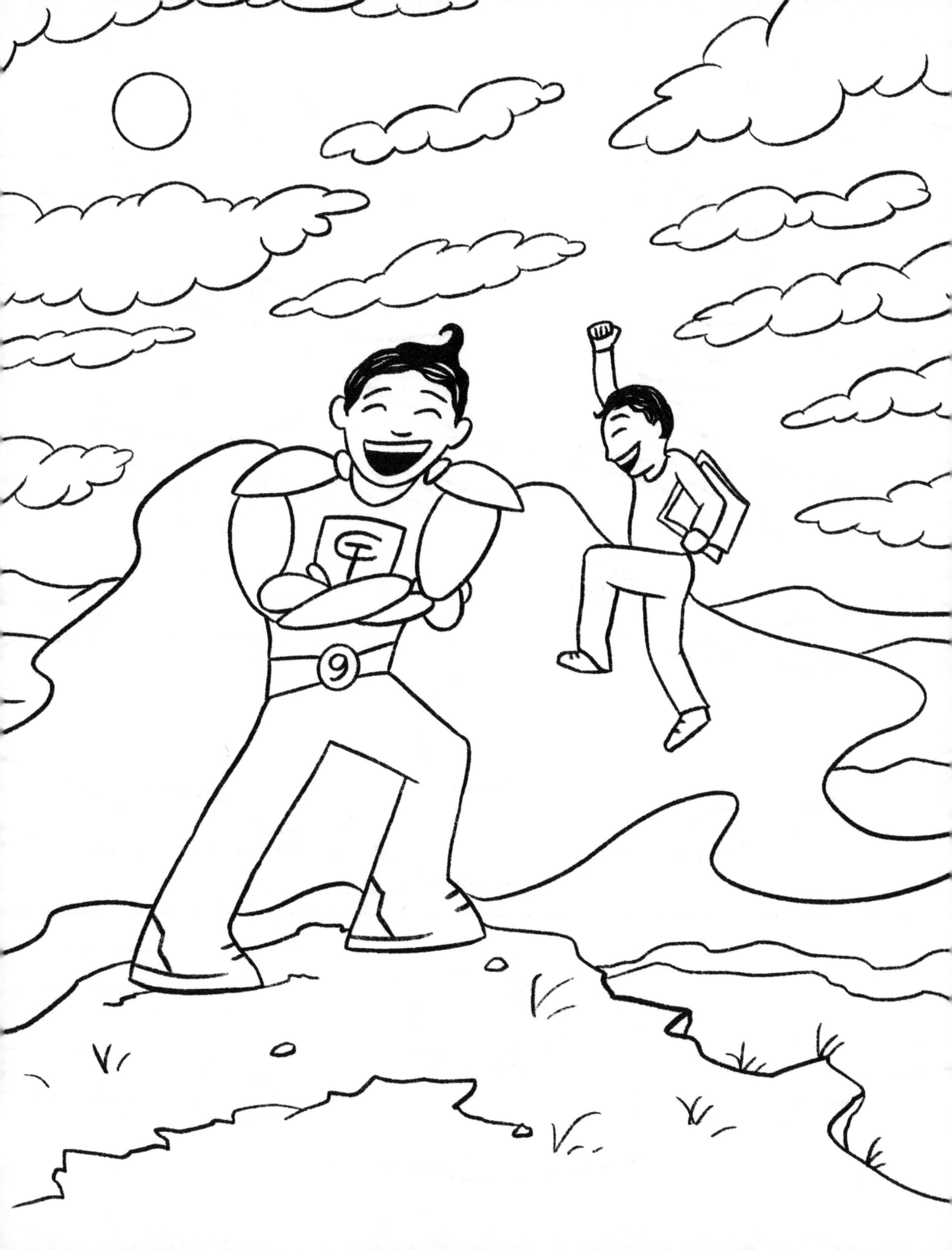

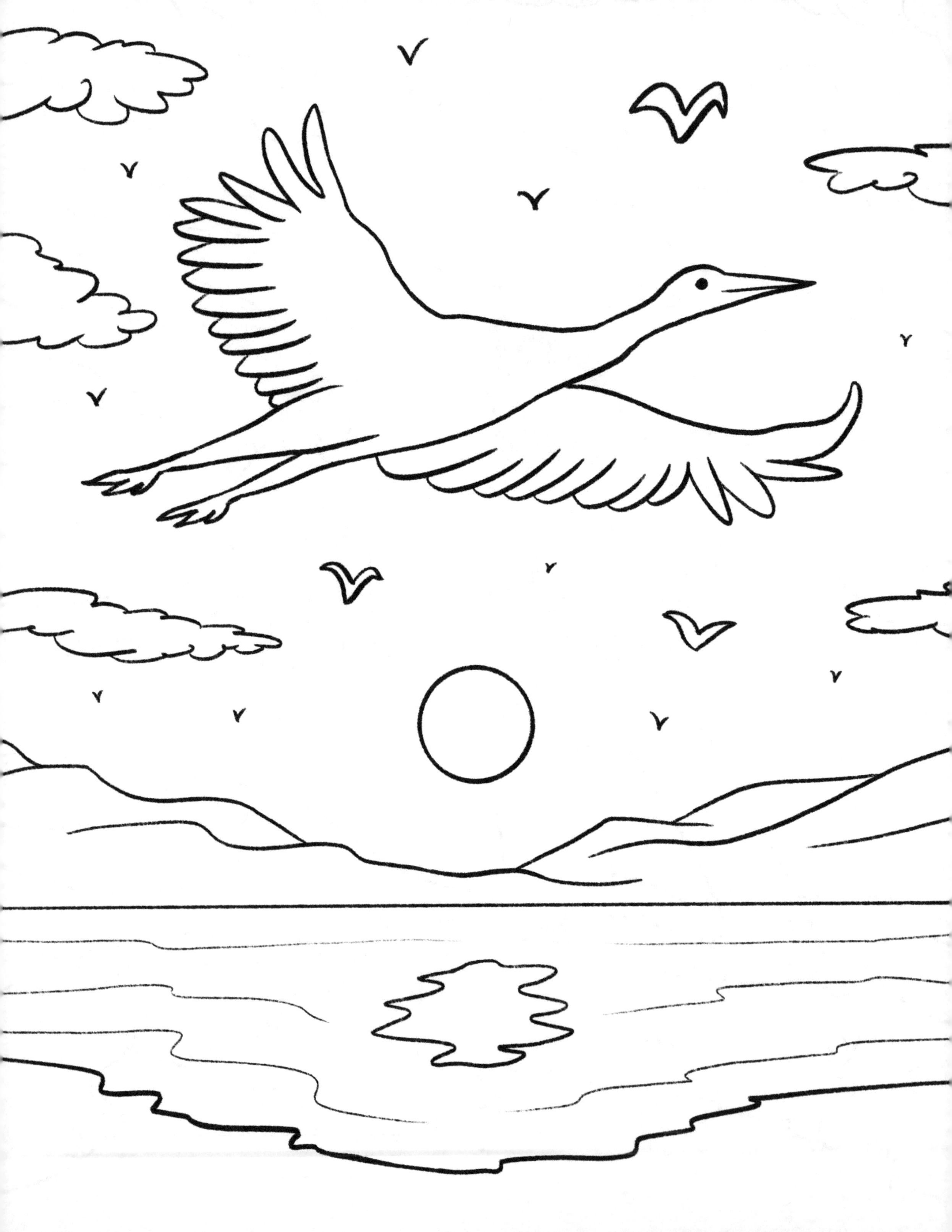

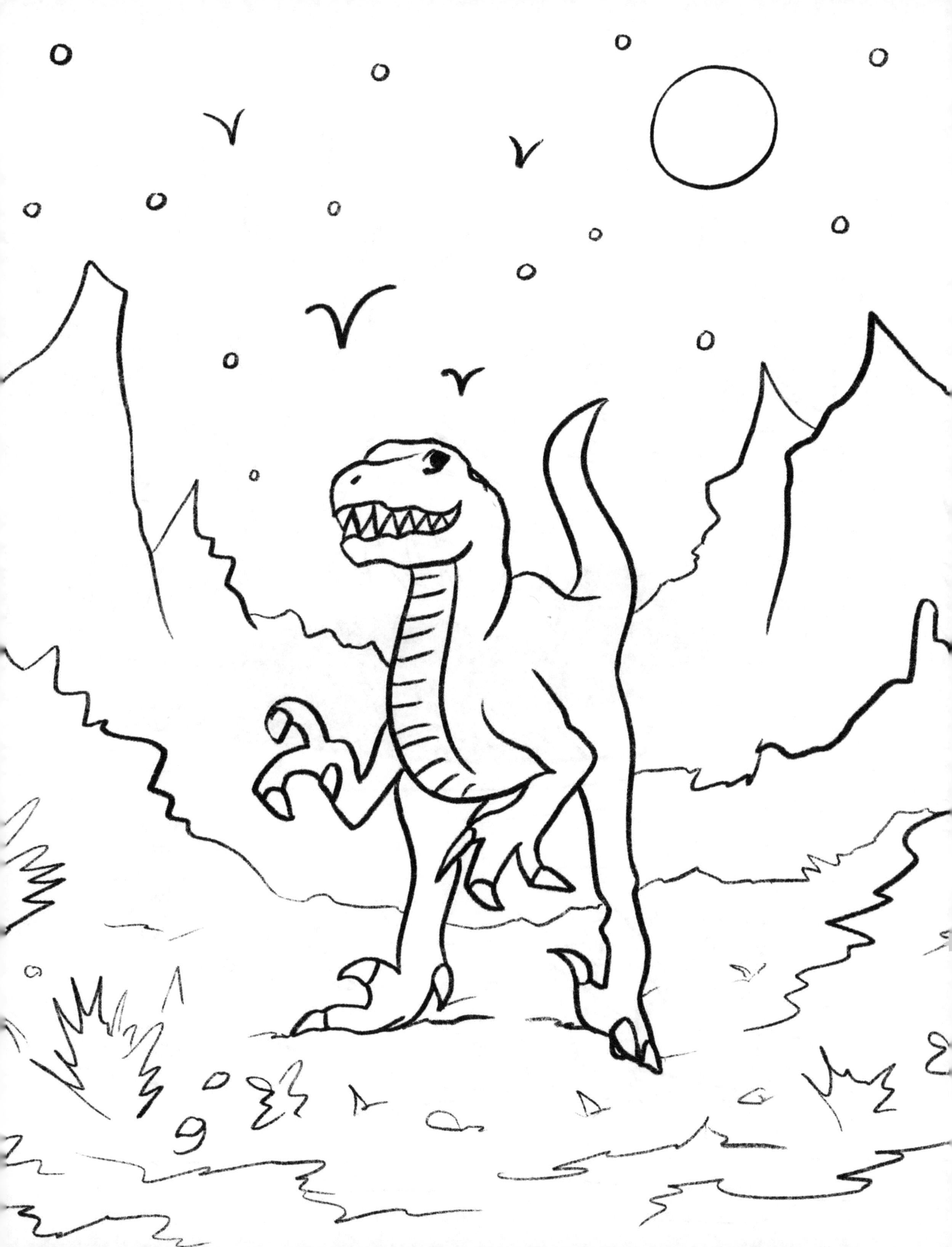

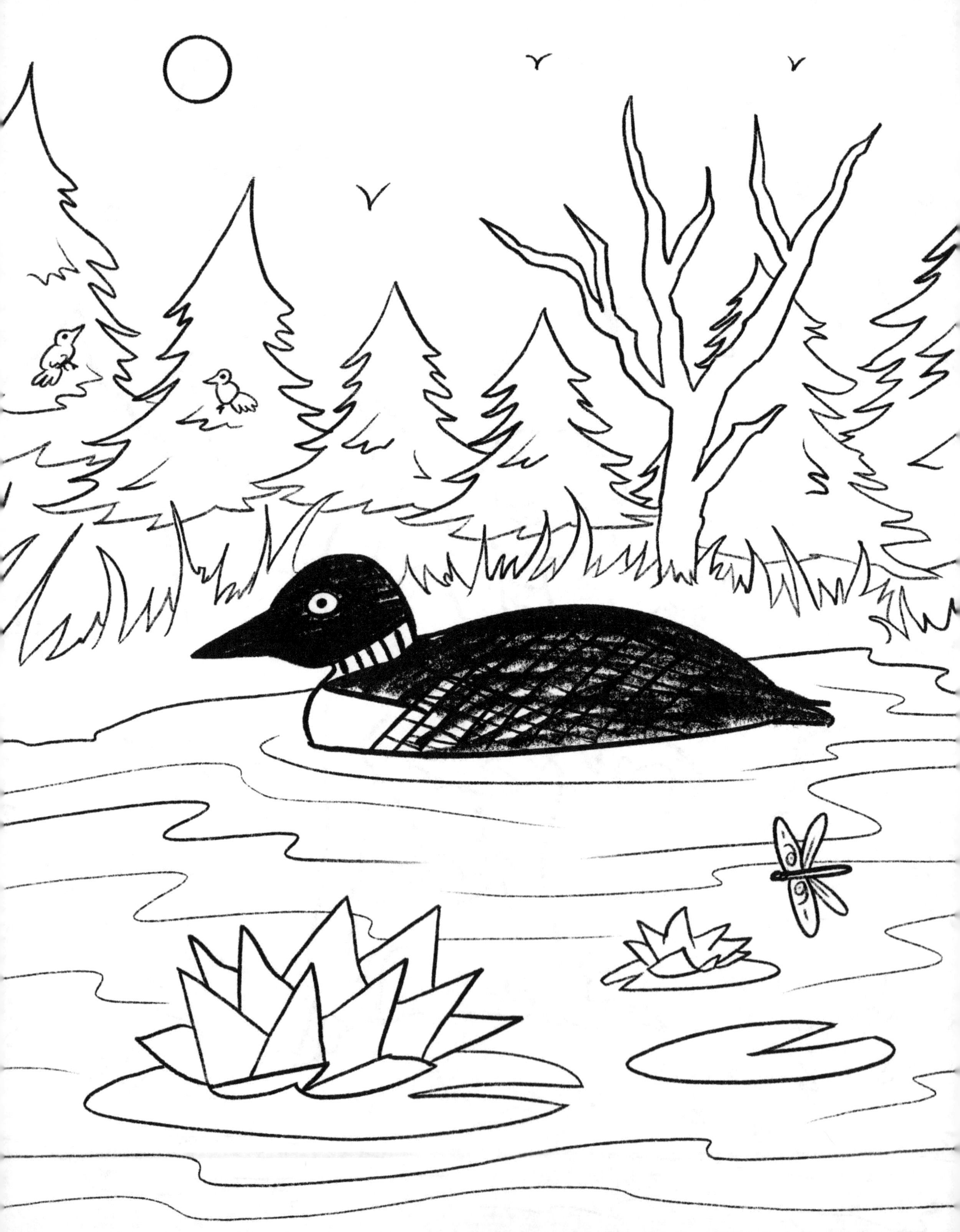

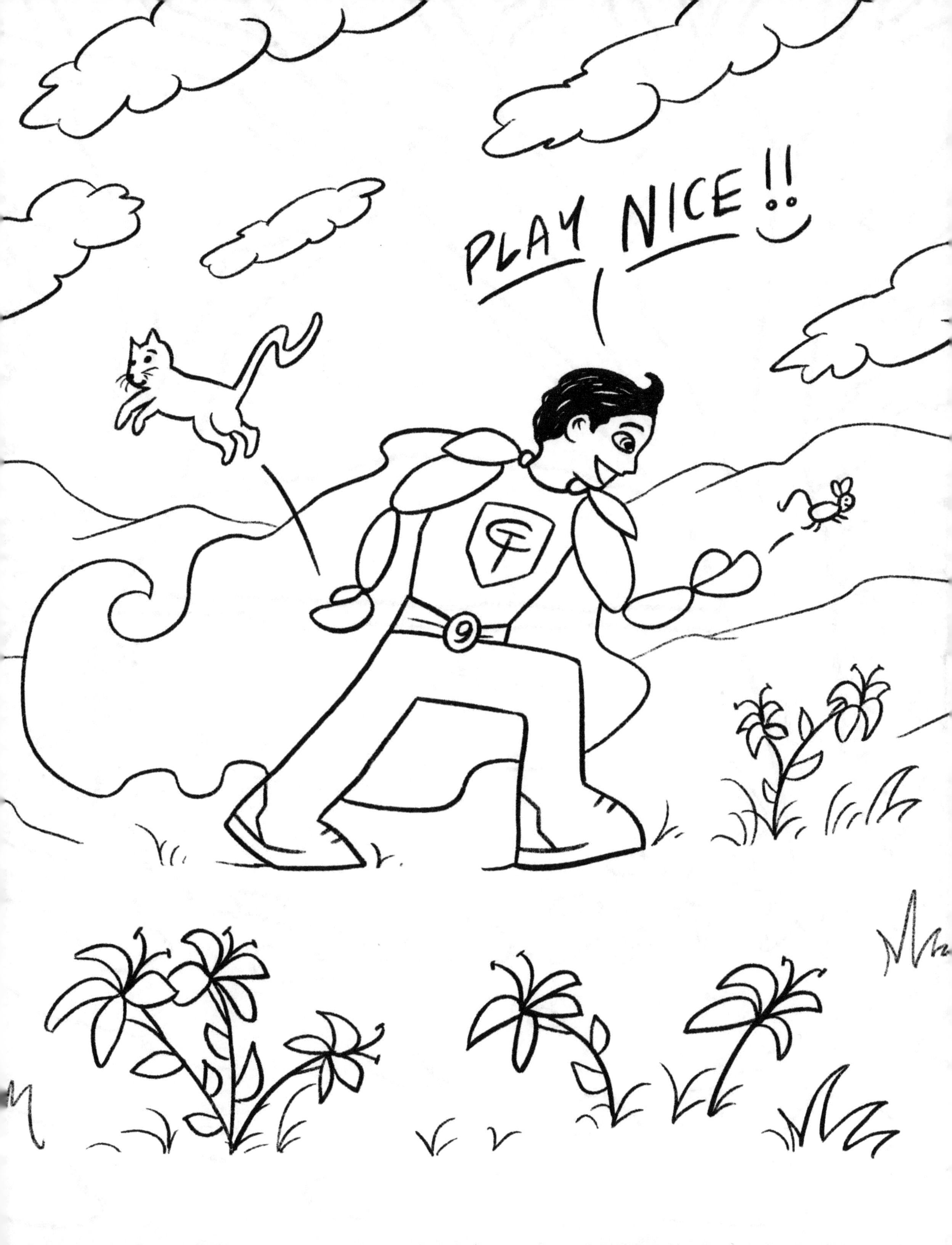
PLAY NICE !!

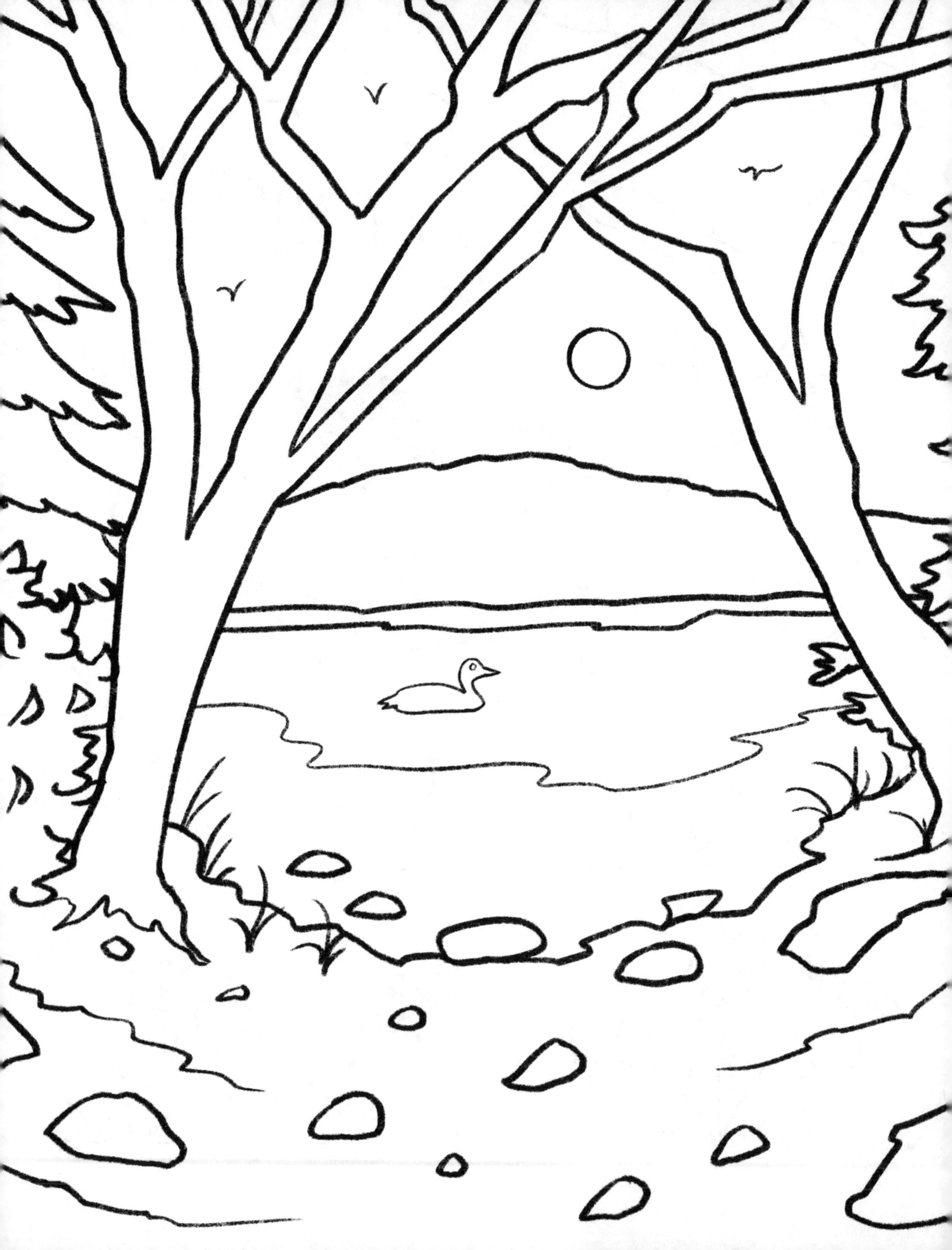

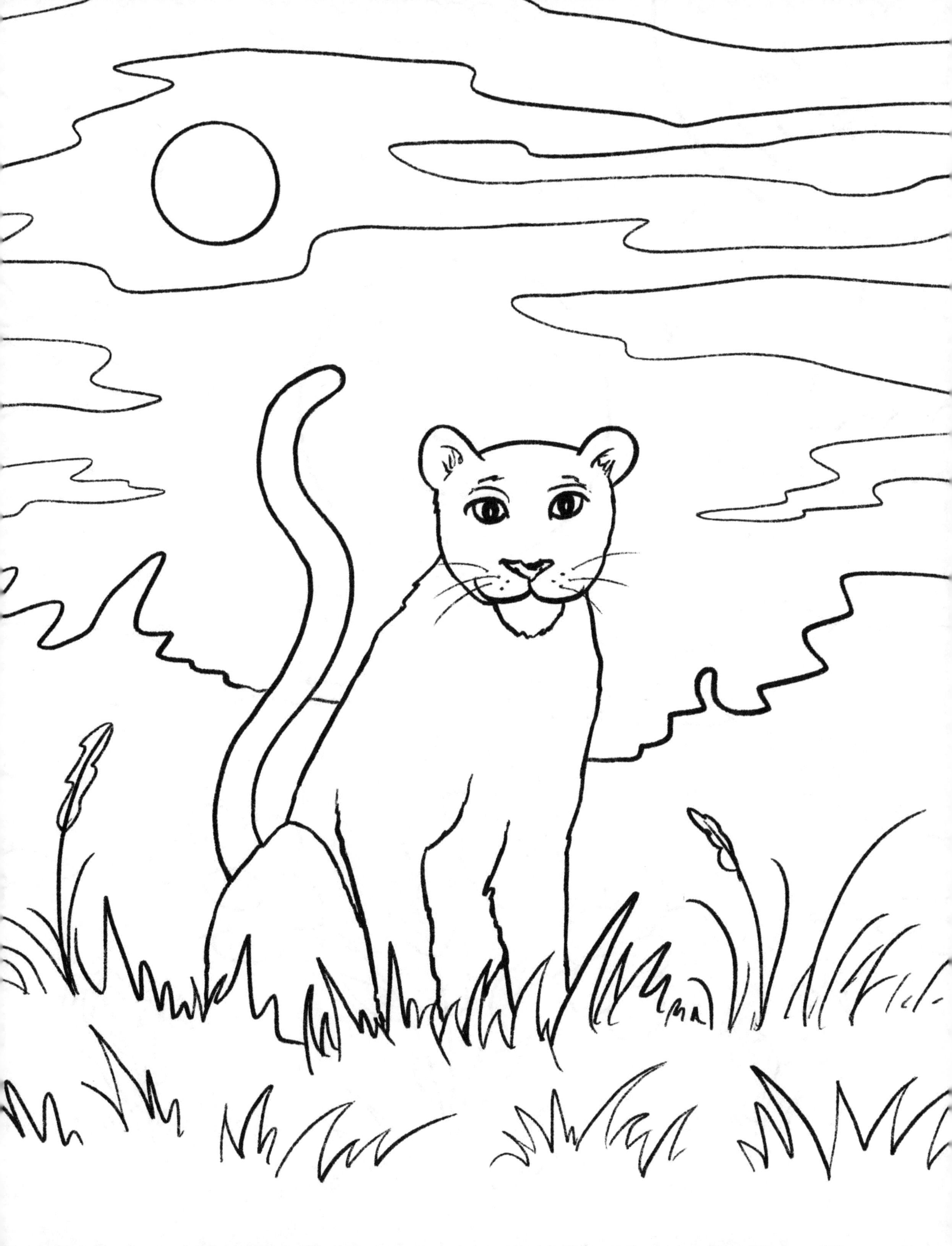

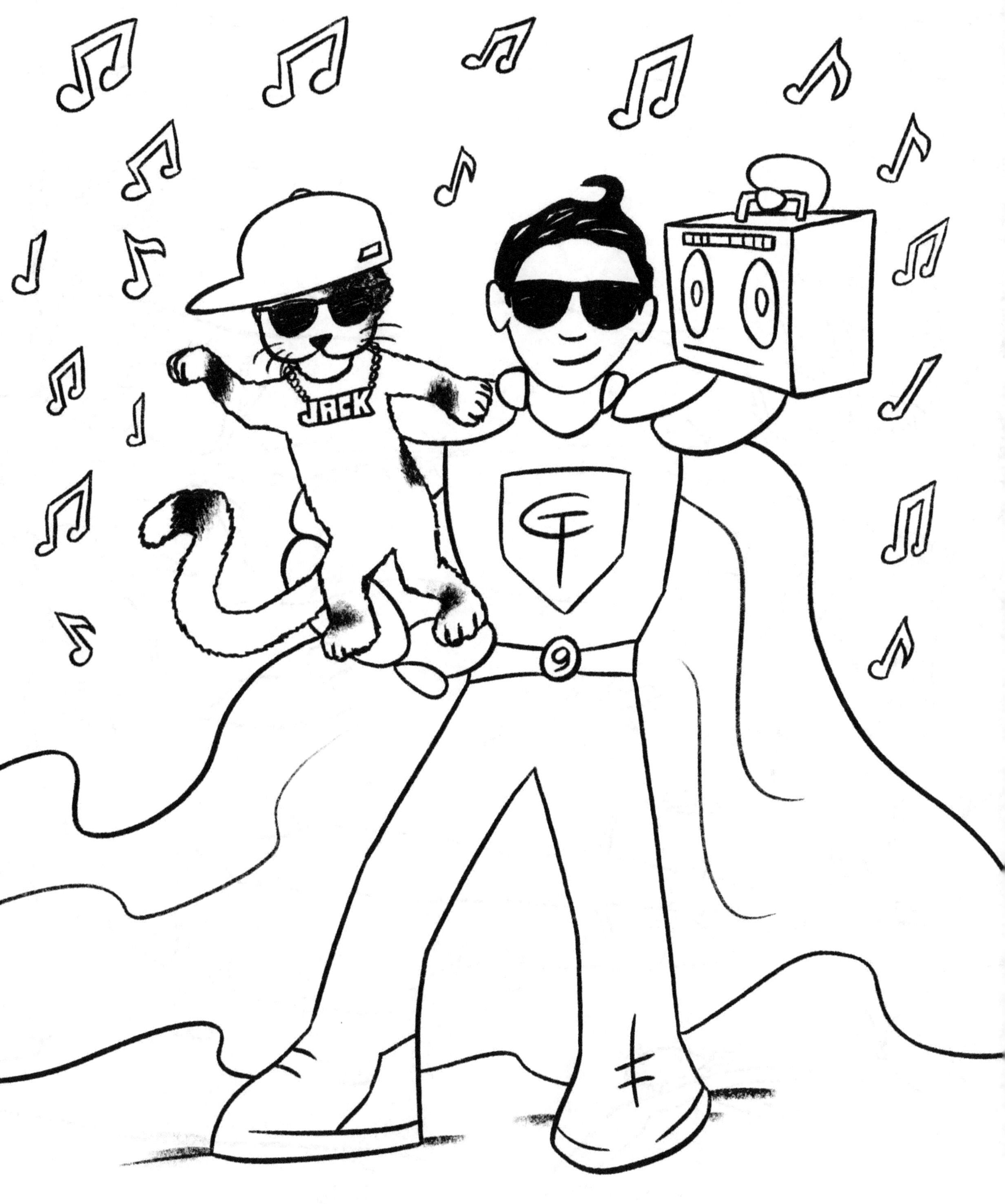
JACK

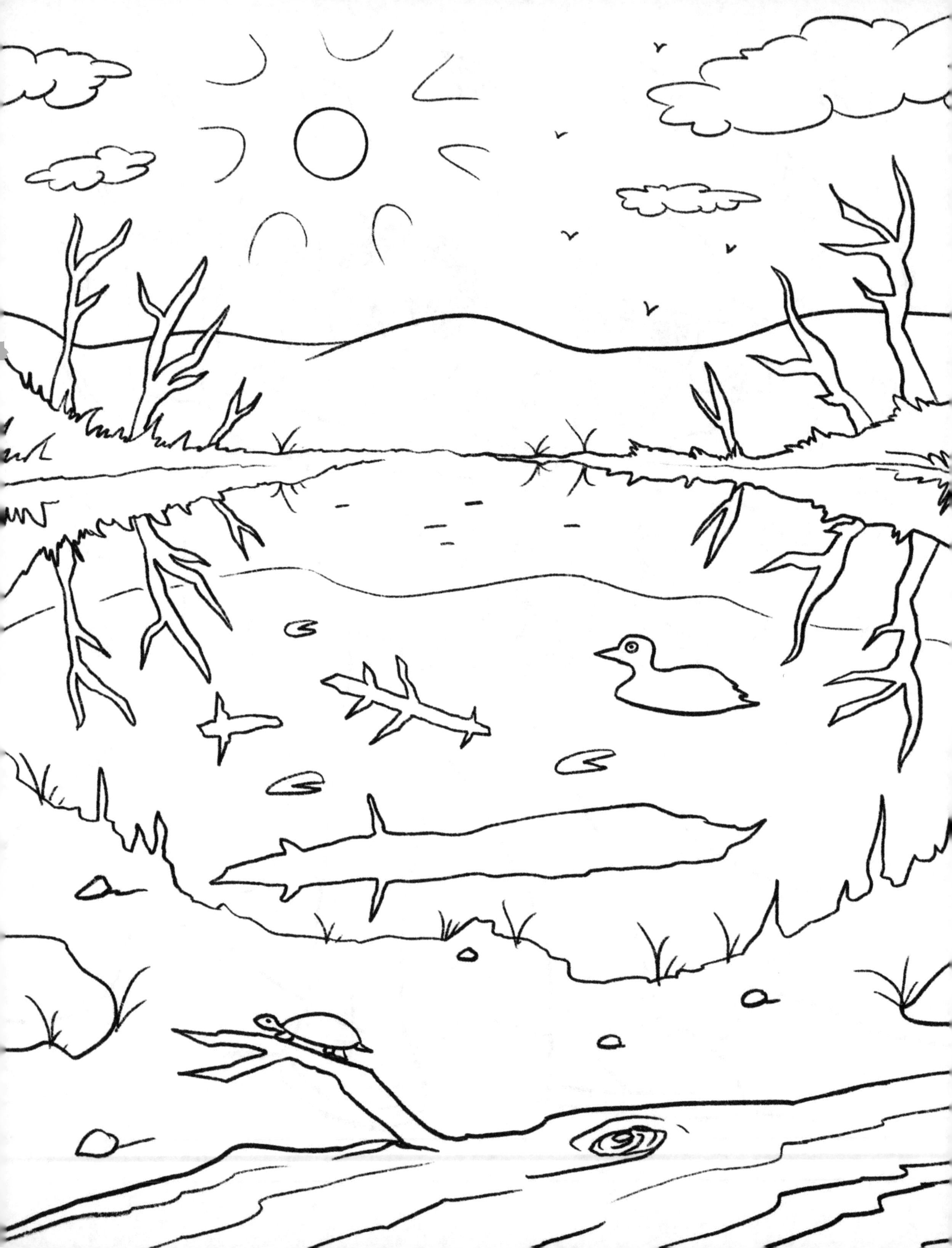

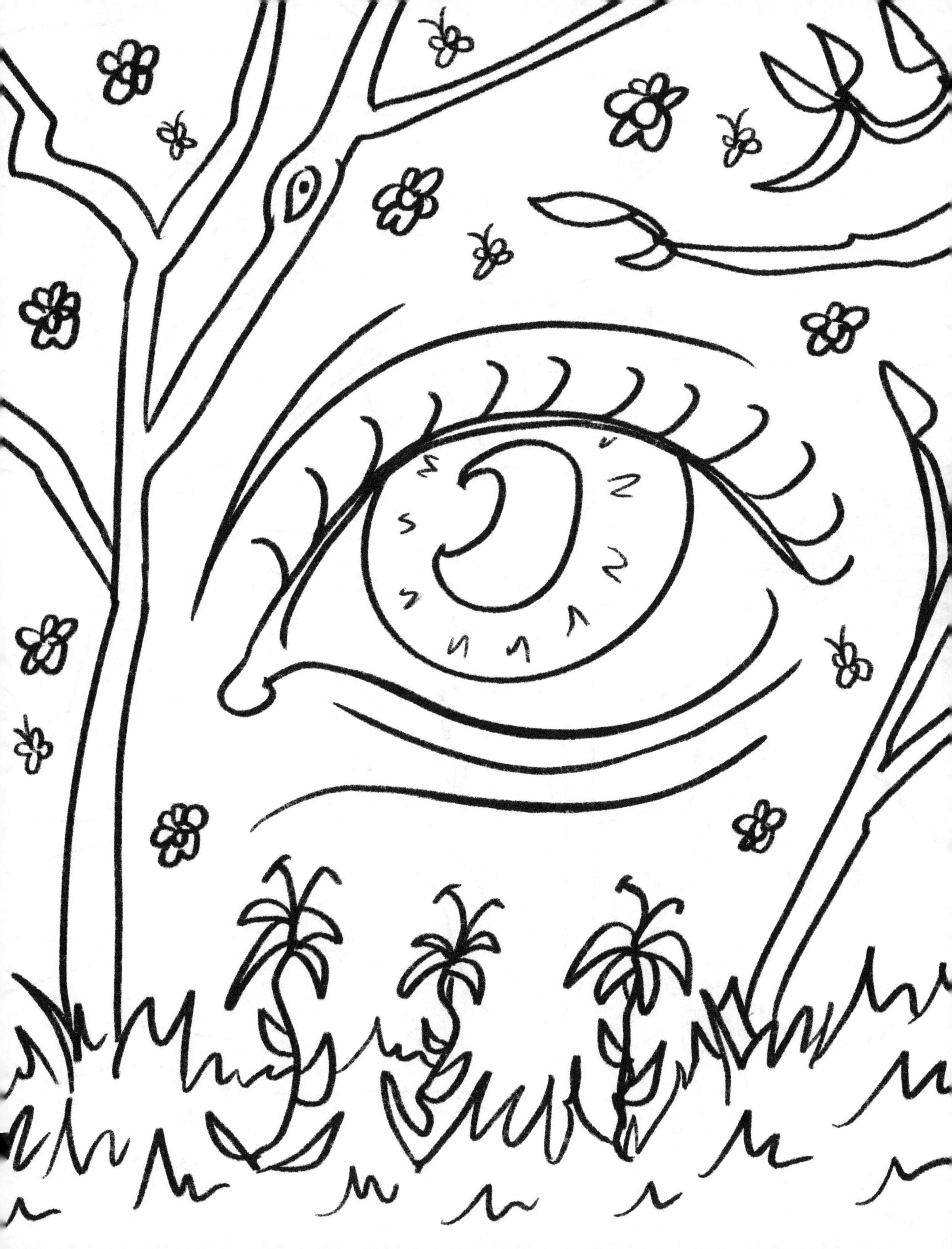

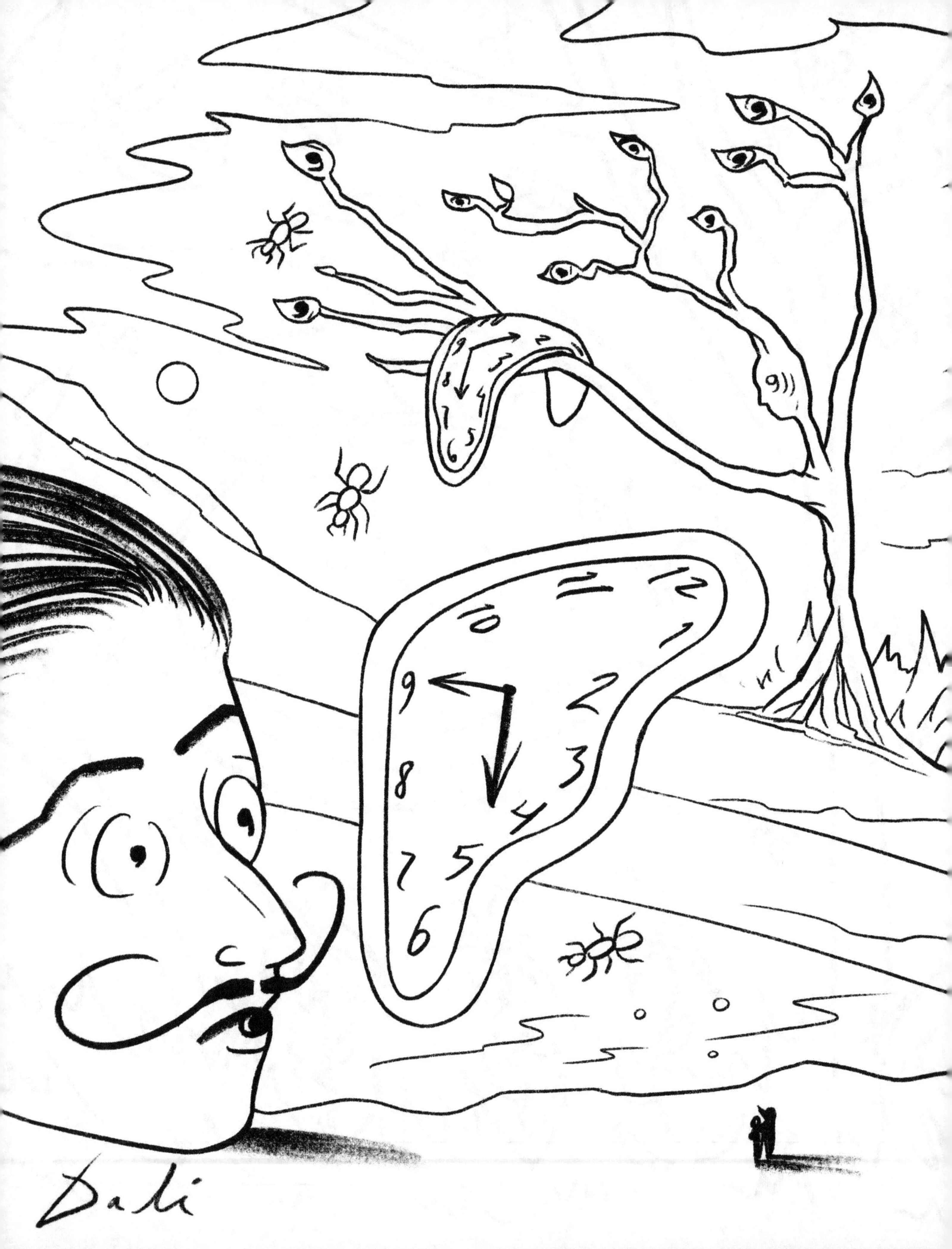
Dali

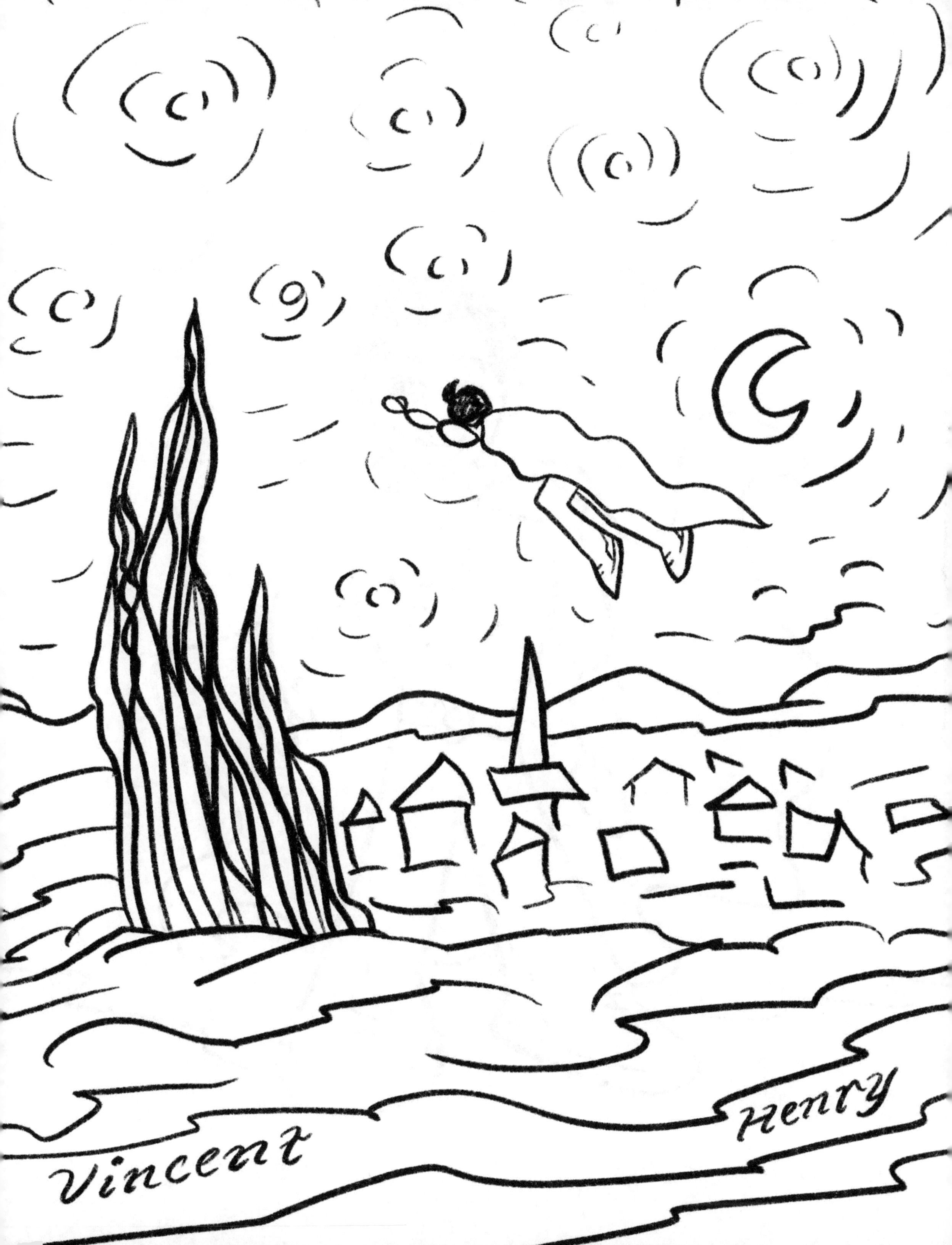
Henry
Vincent

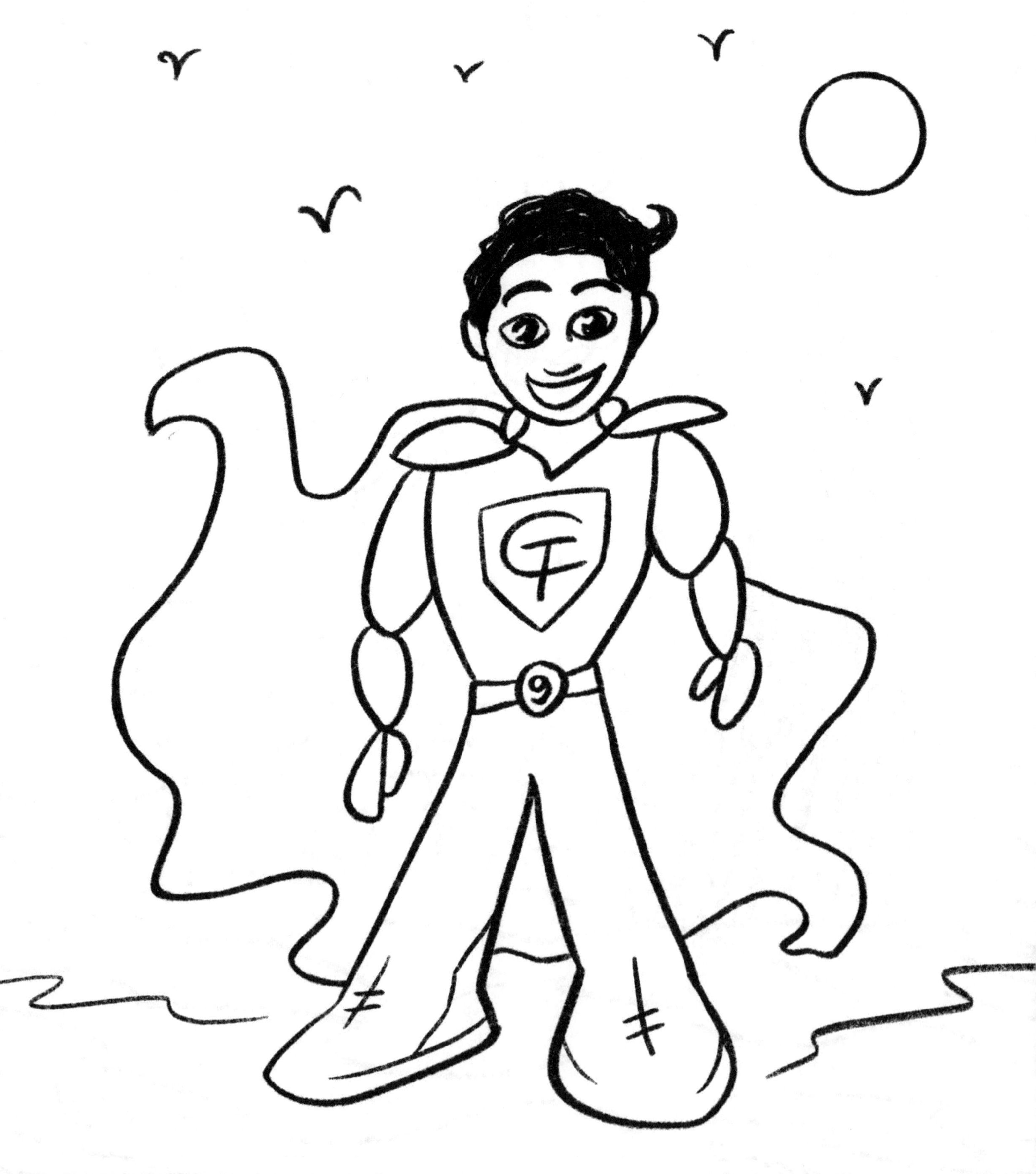

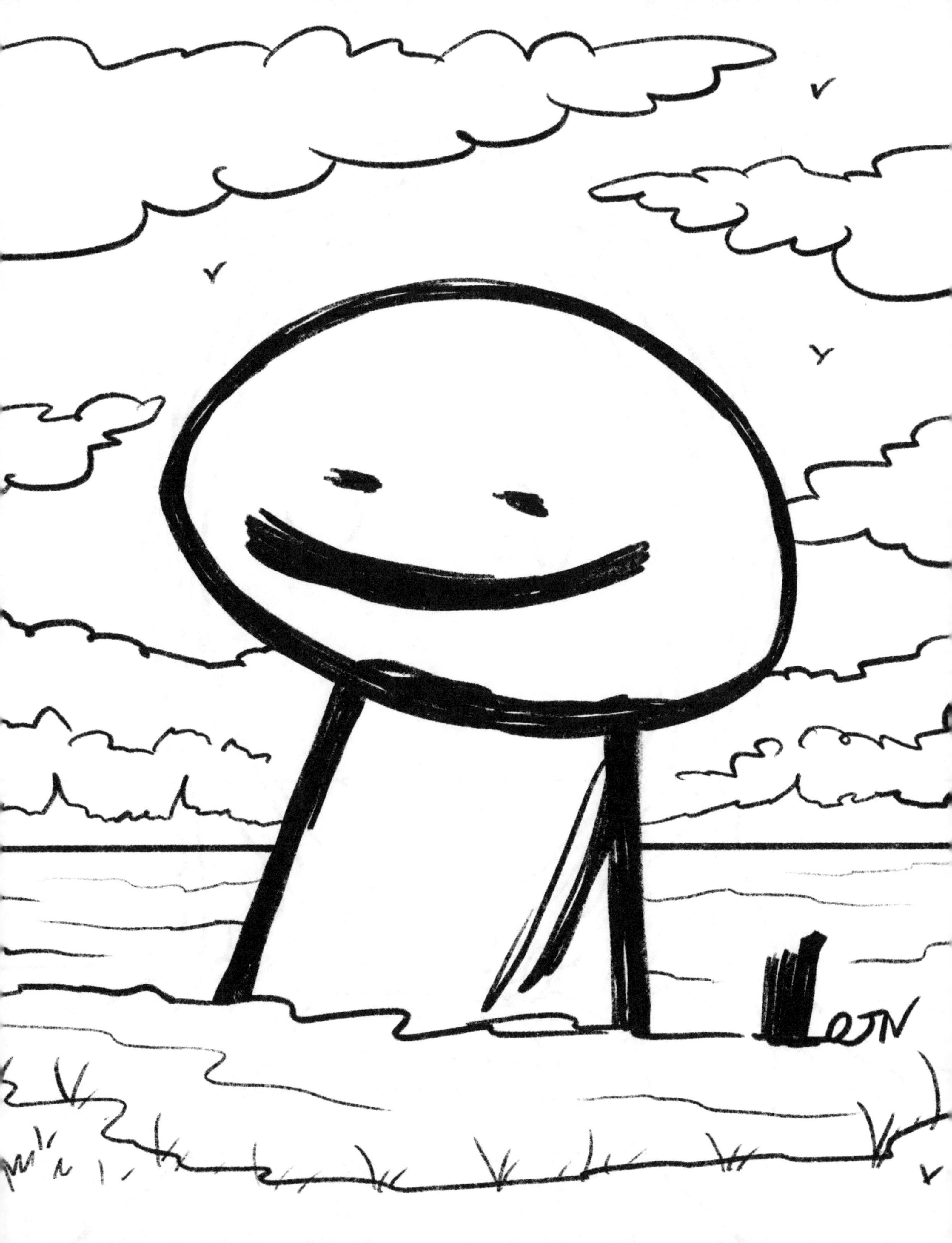

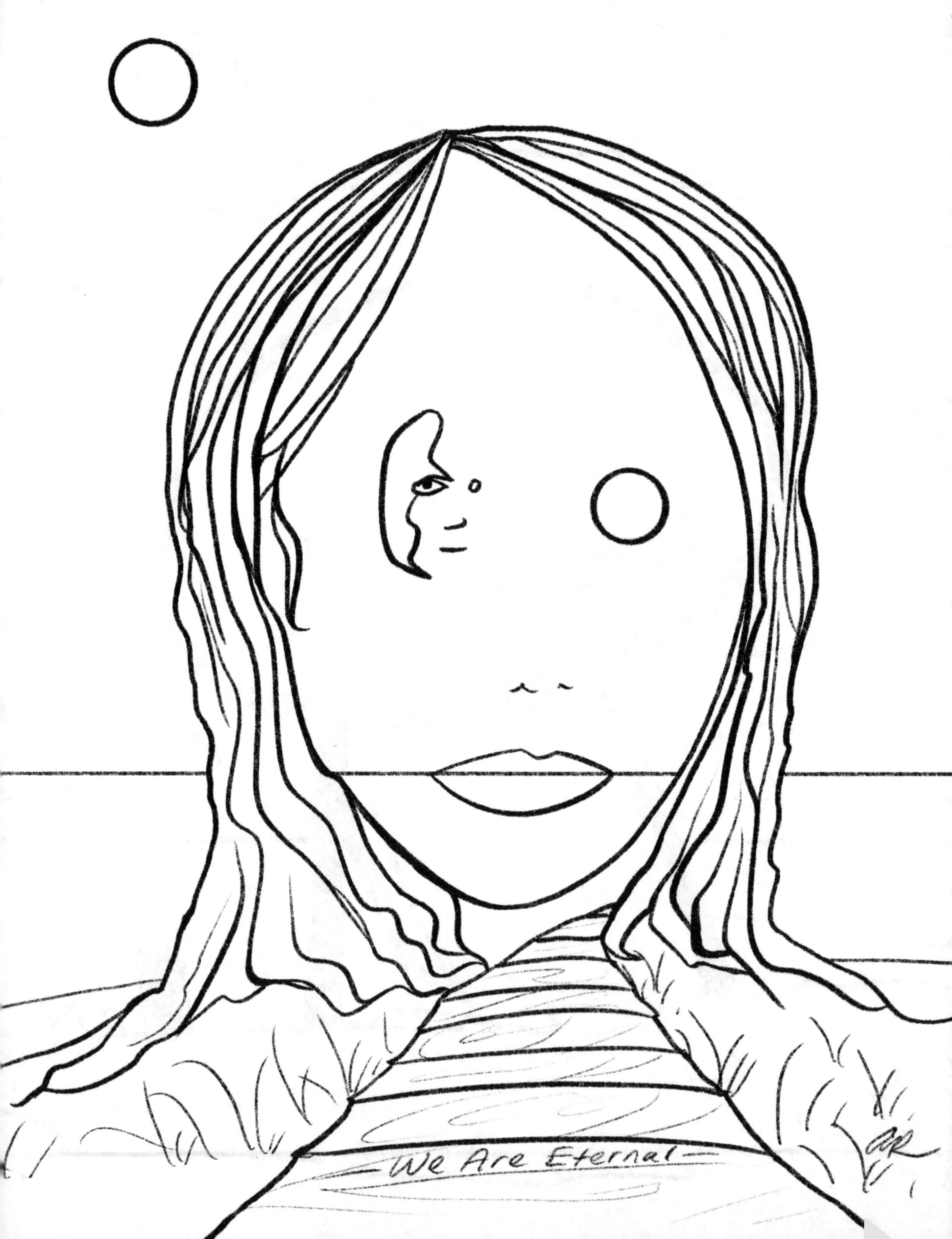
We Are Eternal

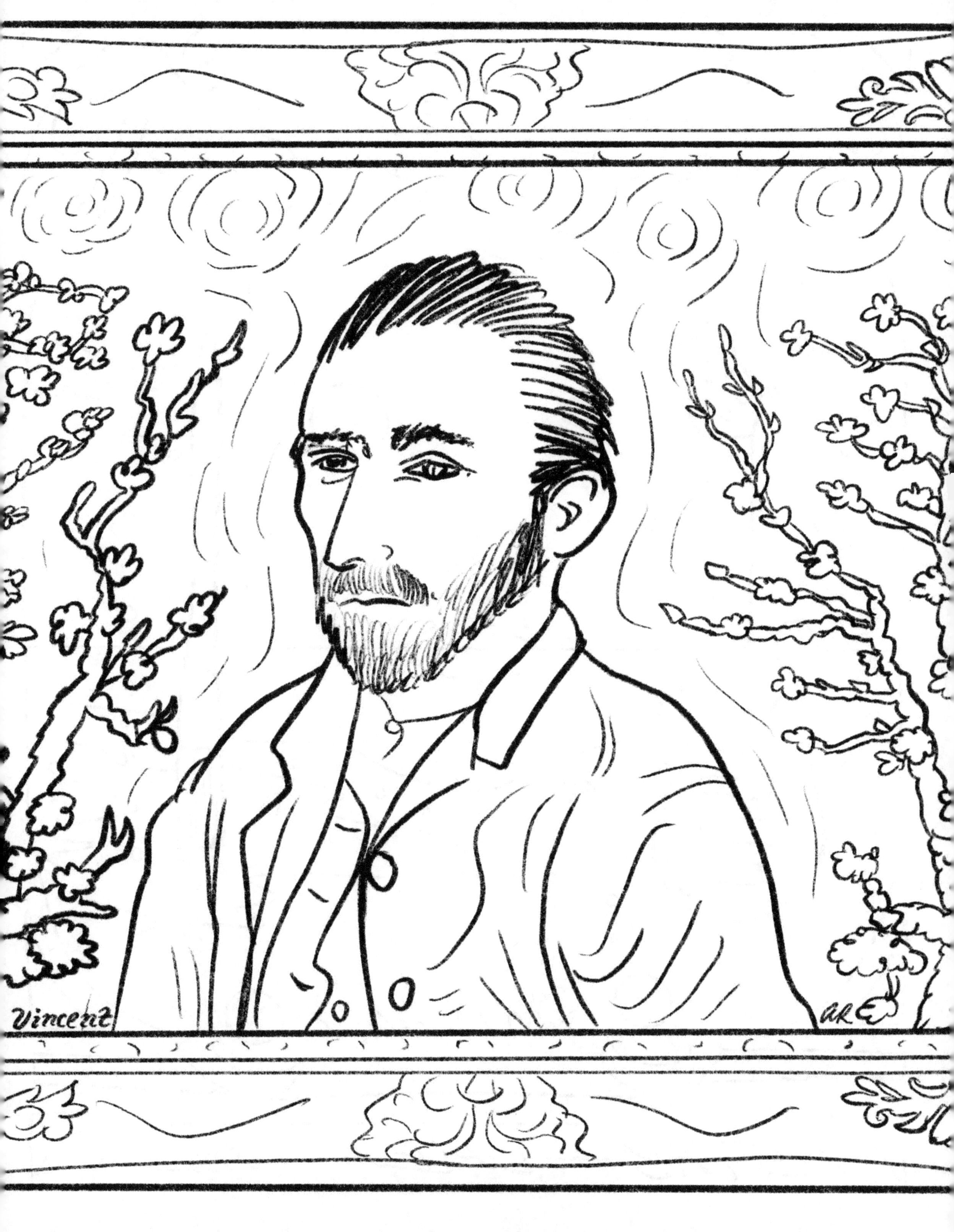
Vincent

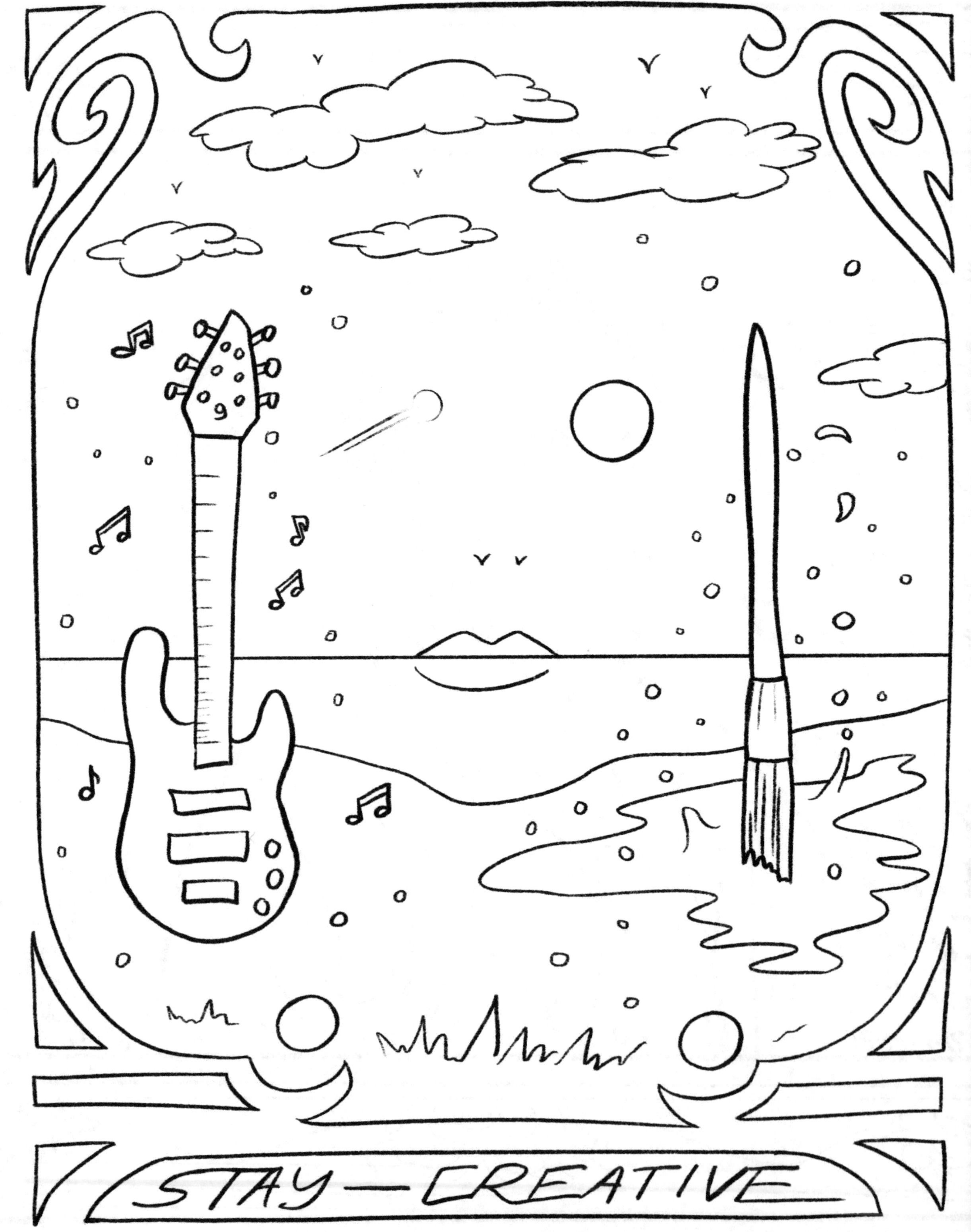
STAY—CREATIVE

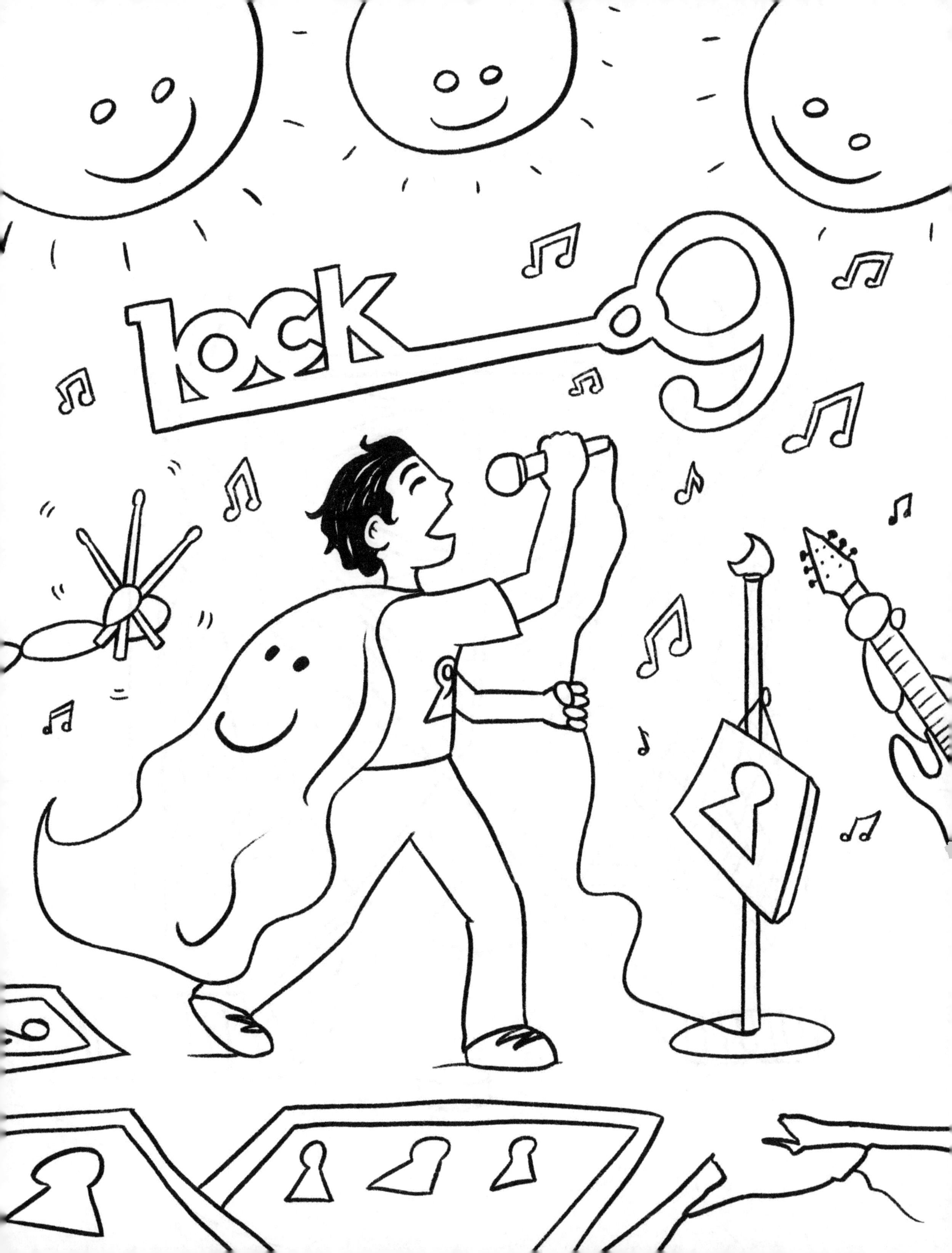
lock

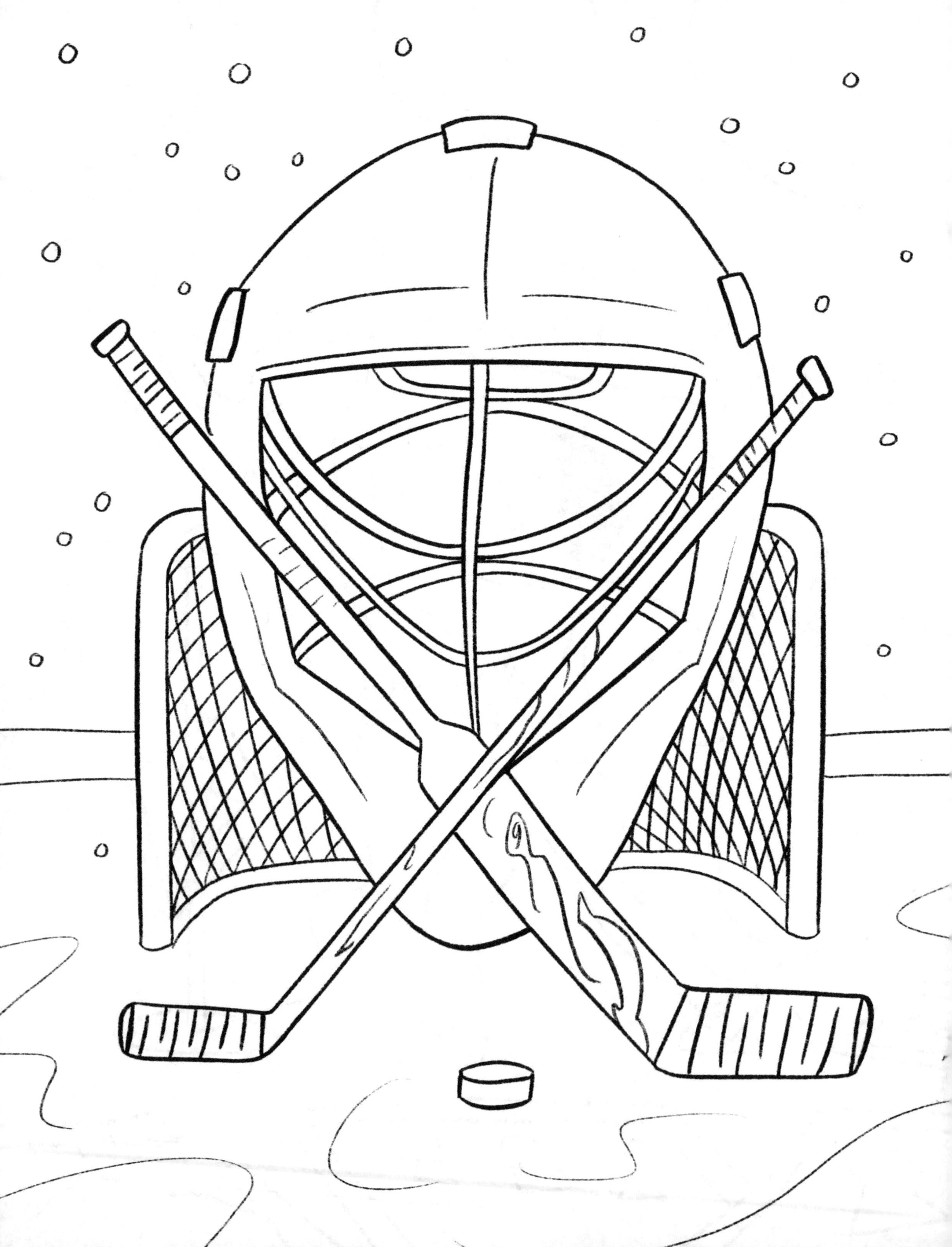

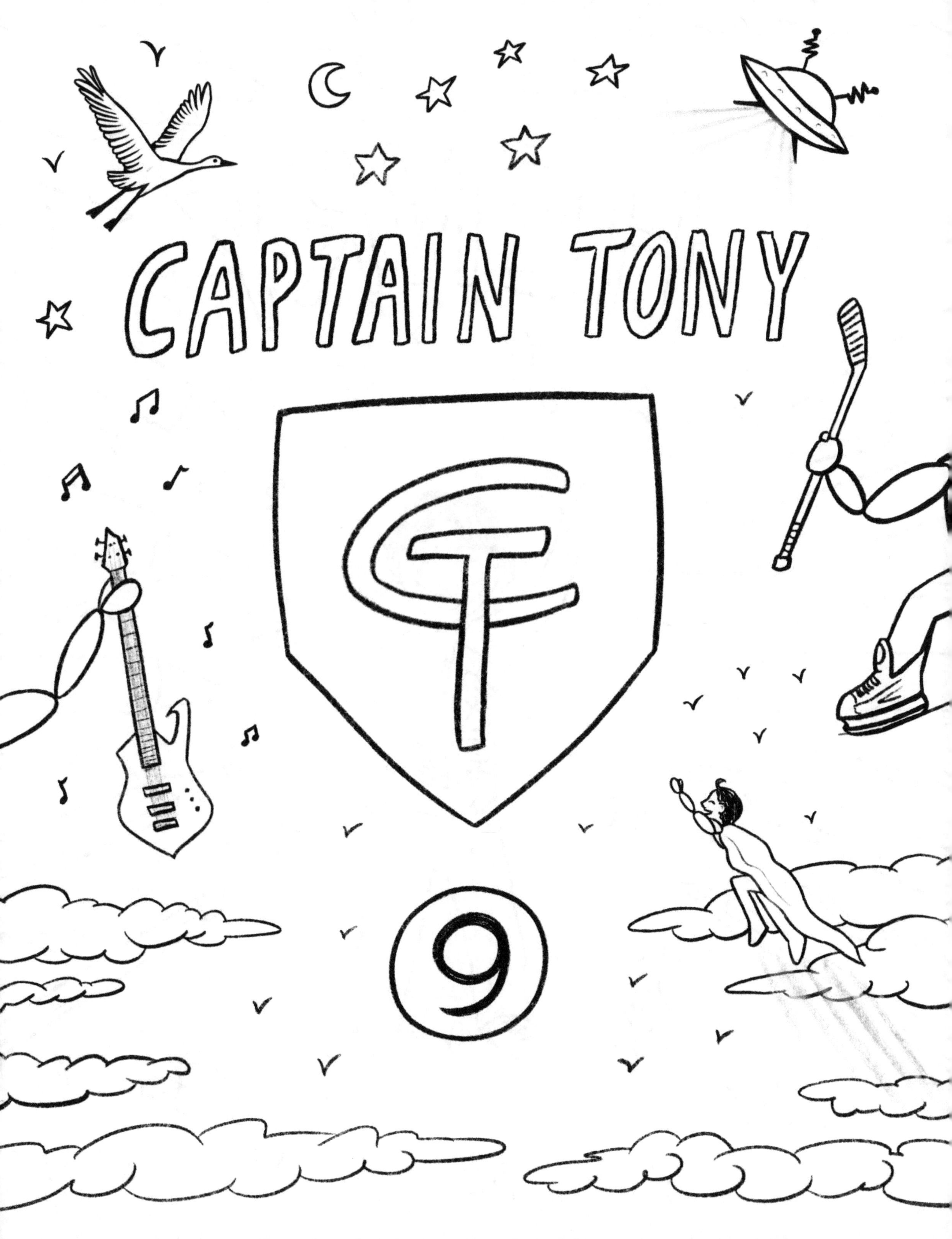
CAPTAIN TONY
CT
9

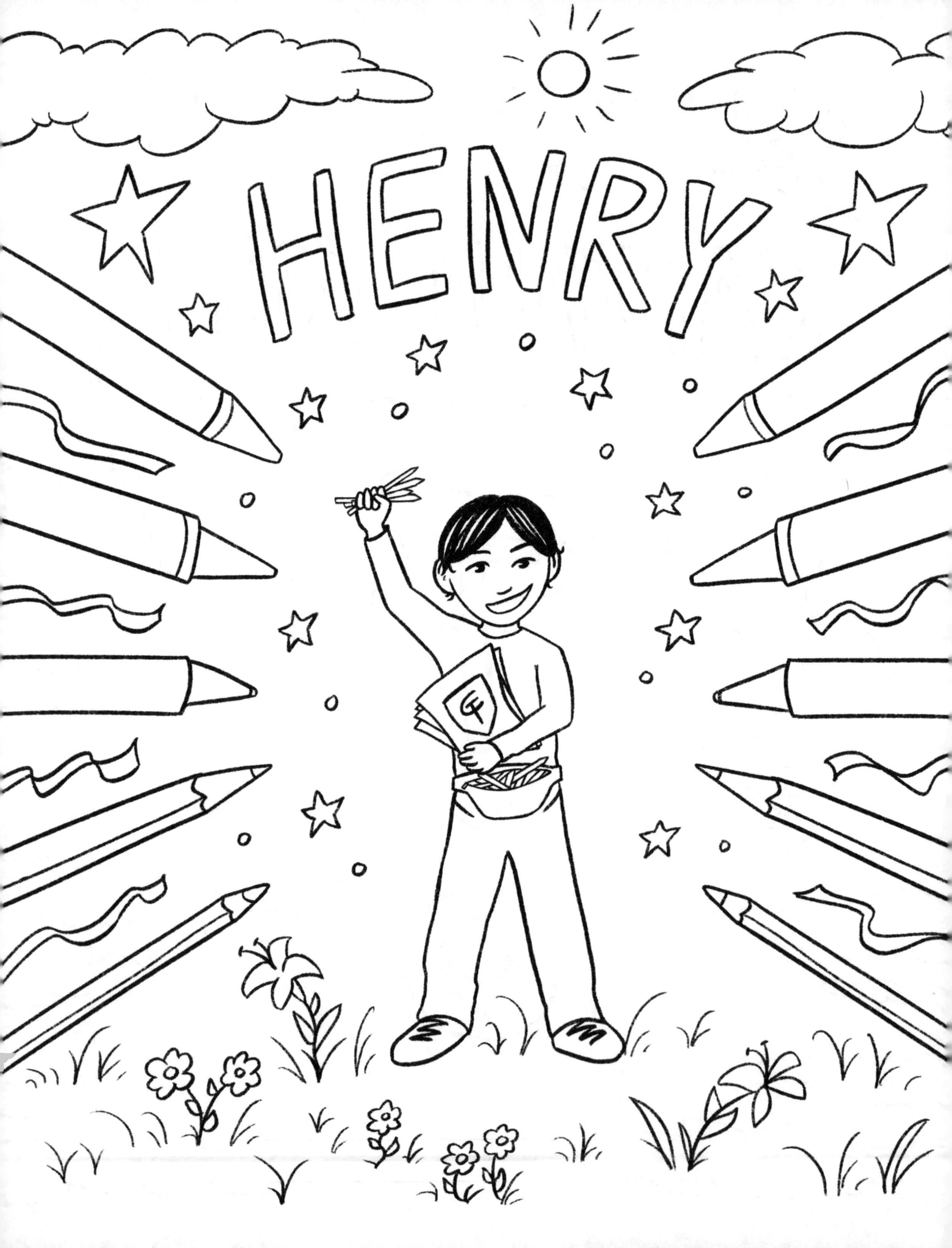
HENRY

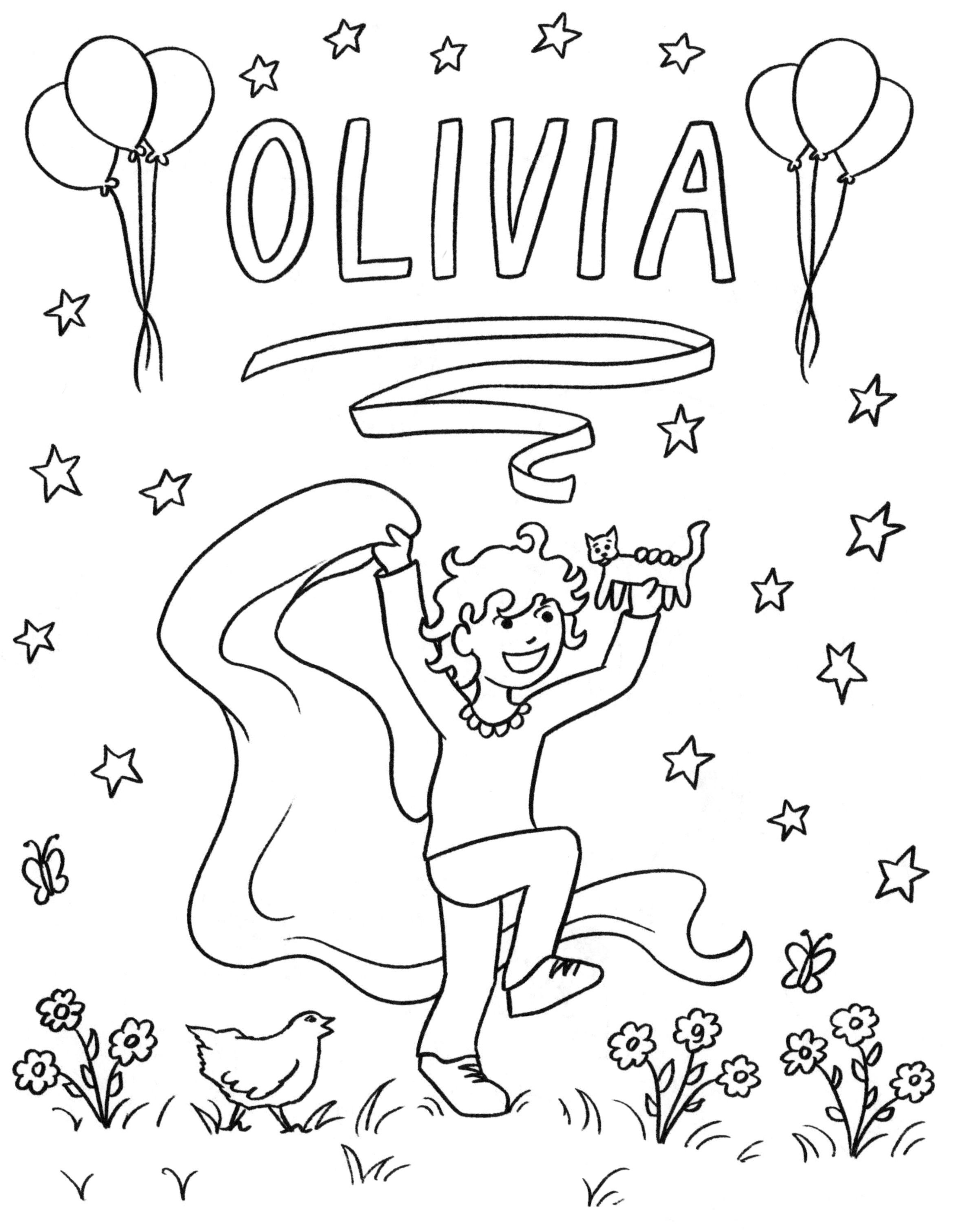
OLIVIA

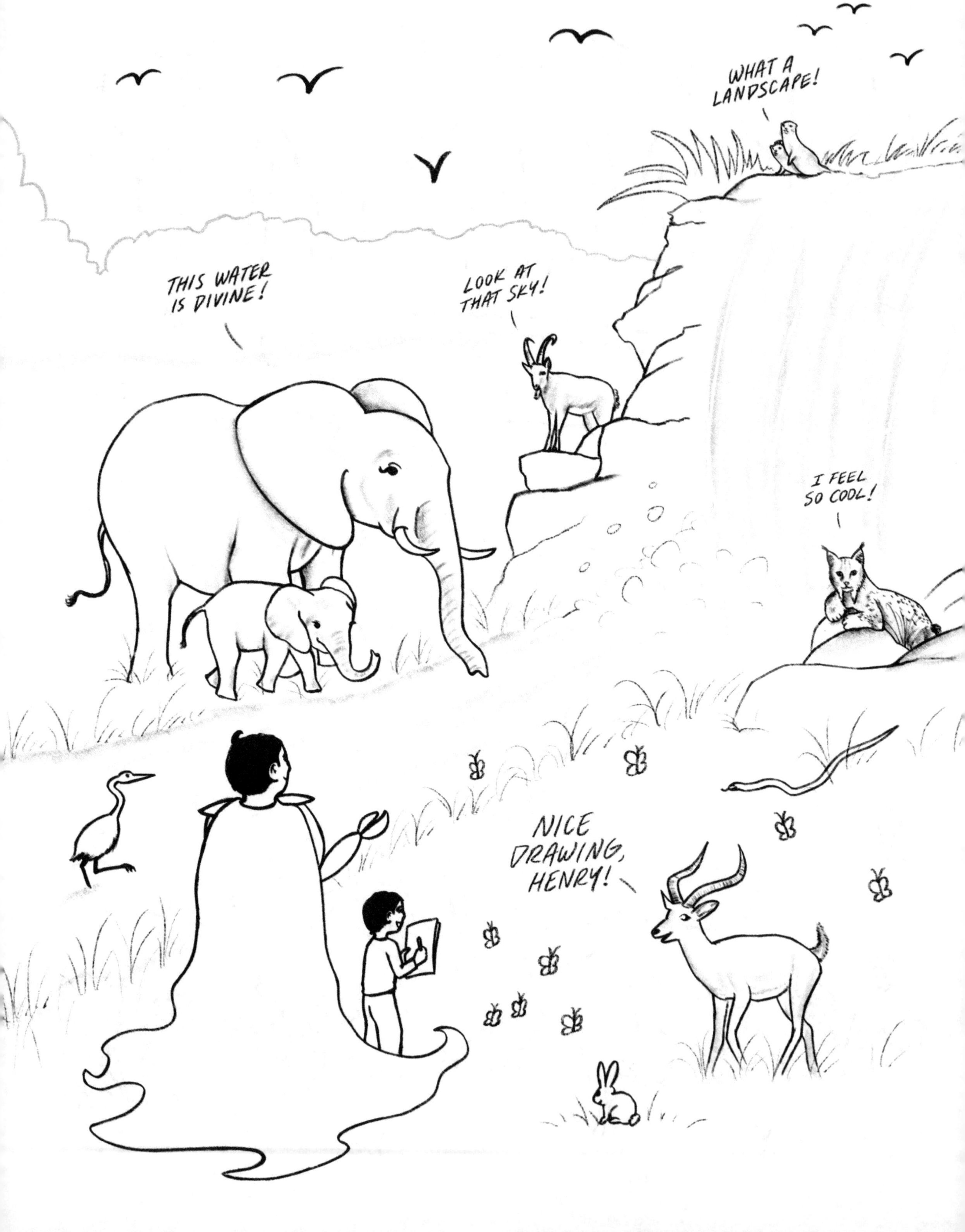

WHAT A LANDSCAPE!

THIS WATER IS DIVINE!

LOOK AT THAT SKY!

I FEEL SO COOL!

NICE DRAWING, HENRY!

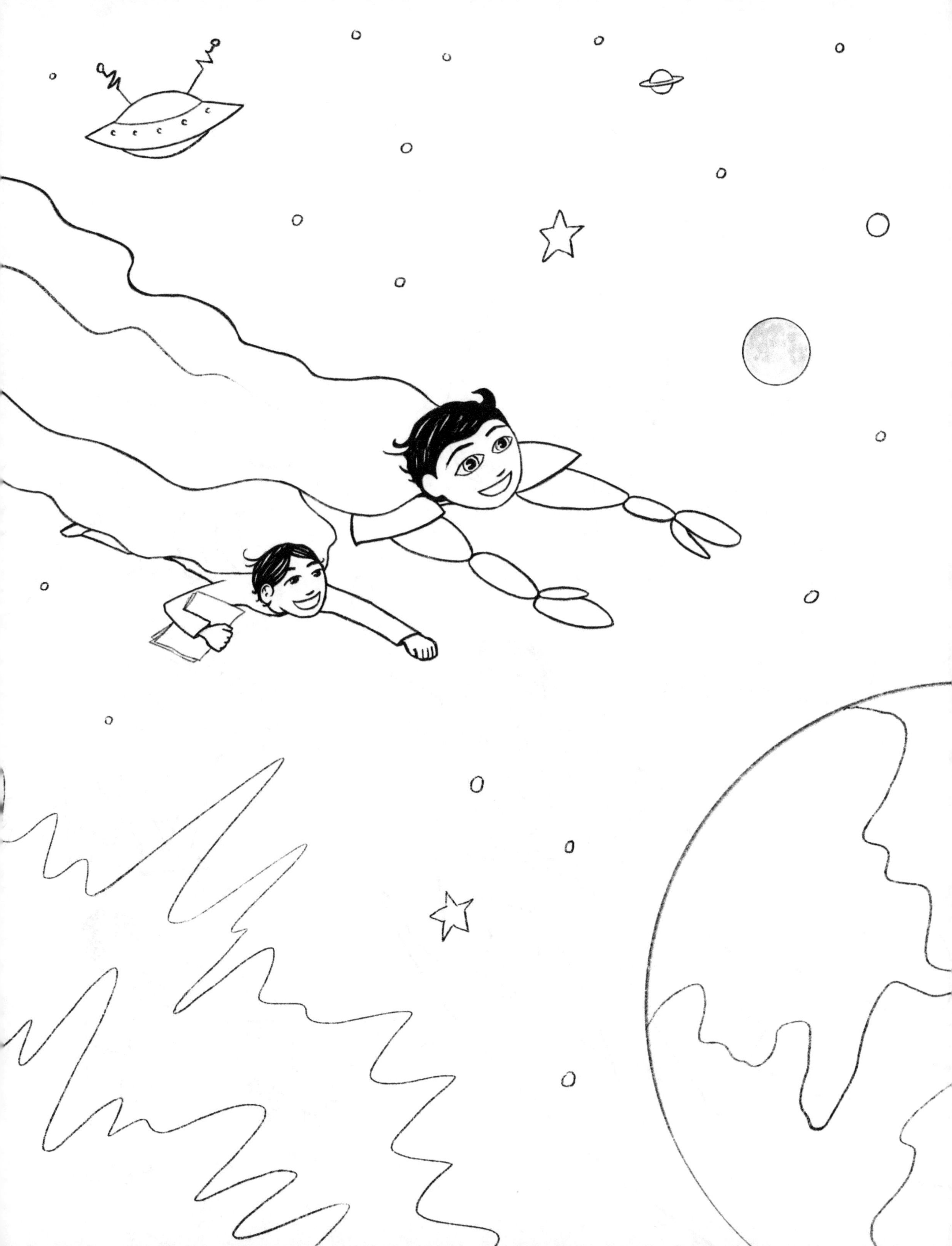

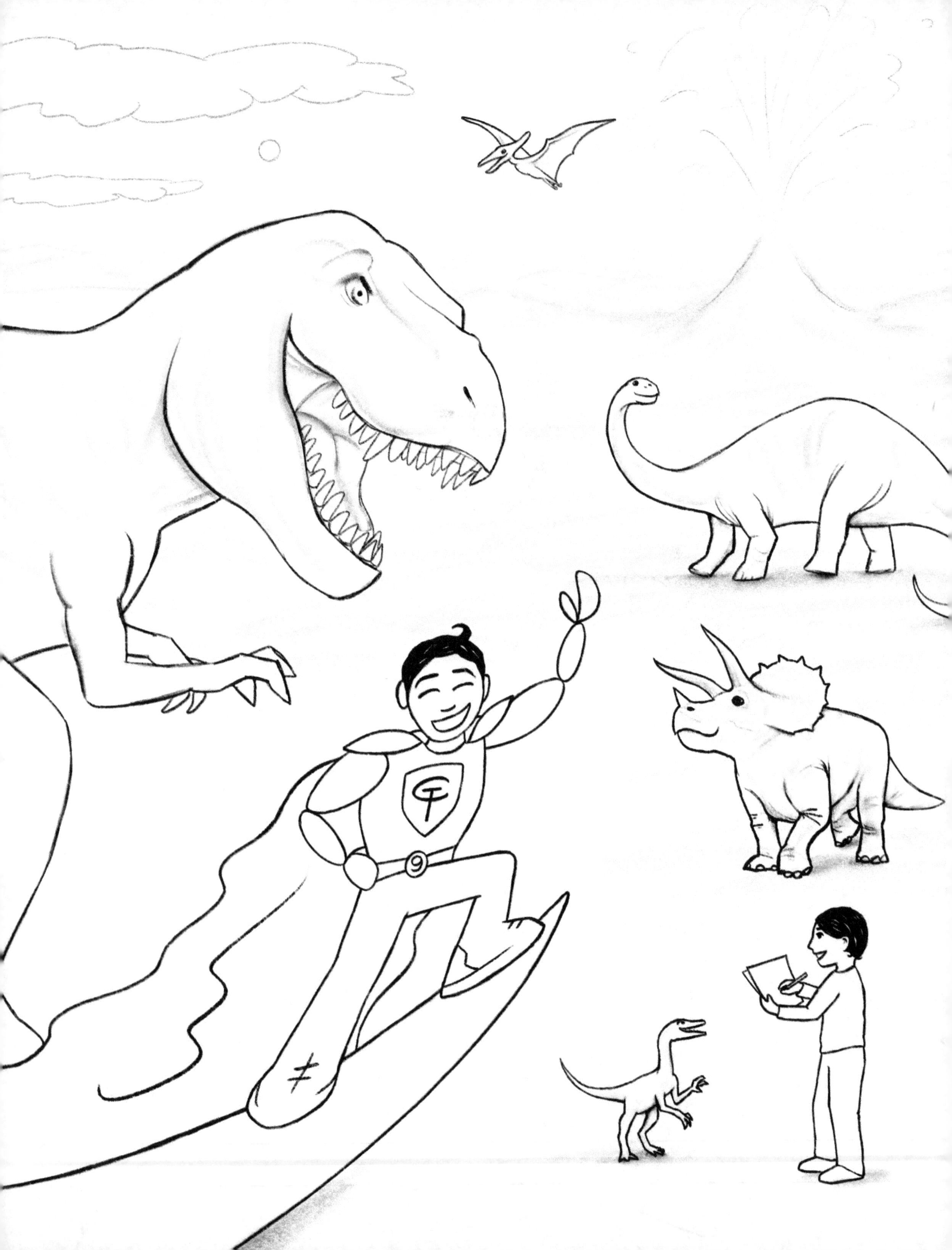

COLORWORLD

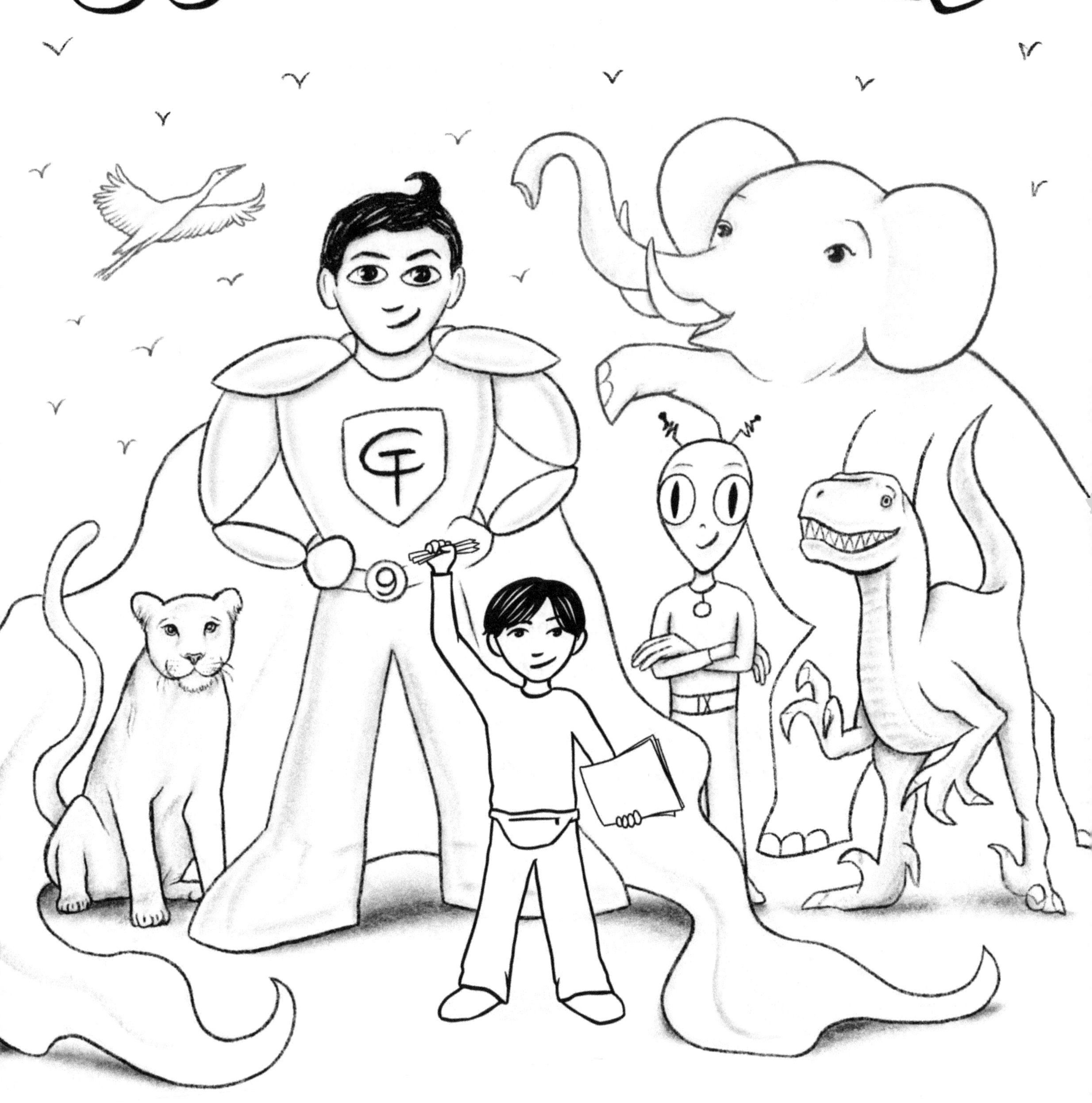

Published in 2022 by
Saratoga Springs Publishing, LLC
Saratoga Springs, N.Y. 12866
www.SaratogaSpringsPublishing.com
Printed in the United States of America

ISBN-13: 978-1-955568-18-0
ISBN-10: 1-955568-9

Written by Anthony Richichi
Illustrations & Graphic Design by Anthony Richichi
Publisher & Design Consultant by Vicki Addesso Dodd

Saratoga Springs Publishing's books are available at a discount when purchased in quantity for promotions, fundraising and educational use.
For more information, contact
colorworld.adventures@gmail.com

Thank you for joining me
to add color to this World!

Stay creative, believe in yourself,
and I'll see you next time!

Anthony J Richichi

www.ingramcontent.com/pod-product-compliance
Lightning Source LLC
LaVergne TN
LVHW081425110826
845149LV00010B/1870

9781955568180